CW01024171

QUEENSLAND
WOMEN IN RUGBY

THE FIRST TWO YEARS 1996-1997

Coach CW (Tasi) Woodard

Published in Australia by Sid Harta Books & Print Pty Ltd,
ABN: 34632585293
23 Stirling Crescent, Glen Waverley, Victoria 3150 Australia
Telephone: +61 3 9560 9920, Facsimile: +61 3 9545 1742
E-mail: author@sidharta.com.au

First published in Australia 2021
This edition published 2021
Copyright © CW (Tasi) Woodard 2021
Cover design, typesetting: WorkingType (www.workingtype.com.au)

The right of CW (Tasi) Woodard to be identified as the
Author of the Work has been asserted in accordance with the
Copyright, Designs and Patents Act 1988.

All rights reserved. No part of this publication may be reproduced, stored in a
retrieval system, or transmitted, in any form or by any means without the prior
written permission of the publisher, nor be otherwise circulated in any form of
binding or cover other than that in which it is published and without a similar
condition being imposed on the subsequent purchaser.

This Manuscript is the property of the author. It should not under any intentions be
copied or reproduced without copyright allowance. Nor should the person engaged
with the document change the content for their personal gain.

CW (Tasi) Woodard
Queensland: Women In Rugby
ISBN: 978-1-925707-57-1
pp188

"We are Queensland.
We are history.
We are family.
We are as one.
We are Queensland.
I am Queensland".

"... with the team in a huddle the last words
spoken before taking the field for every game."
Tasi Woodard

*

'The Sunday Mail' — December 27, 1998

"The Queensland Women's Rugby Union side is one of the state's most successful representative sporting teams. It is also one of our best kept secrets and the players are managing to breakdown a few stereo types along the way."

*

ABOUT THE AUTHOR

Tasi forged a successful playing and coaching career for more than forty years in both the military and civilian rugby environments. With this foundation he was invited by the Queensland Rugby Union (QRU) to select and coach the inaugural Queensland Women's Rugby team for 1996 through to 1998.

From the very beginning the team excelled and could claim to be the best provincial team in world rugby. They did not lose a game and were the first Australian team to defeat an International side, which was second in the world rankings.

He was fortunate to have at his disposal a team of Queenslanders; athletic with outstanding skills and a steely professional attitude, who were equal to anyone representing their state. Their results may never be realised in Australian women's rugby again.

Tasi was awarded the Australian Sports Medal in the year 2000 (struck to commemorate the new millennium) for his dedication and achievements in rugby.

BY THE AUTHOR

F ollowing two years of being involved with women in sport, in my case rugby, my whole attitude towards these athletic individuals had been altered by them in their complete devotion to their chosen sport and their professionalism.

Queensland and Australia are fortunate to possess these sport driven women, strong in character and their amazing endeavour to succeed in their rugby careers.

I wish to thank these outstanding athletes for giving a tutoring, as I had never been involved with women in sport in any capacity and it certainly changed my opinion to women participating and succeeding in such a brutal team sport.

I thank them for my education and my admiration for them will never wane. I feel privileged to have had an association with them.

ACKNOWLEDGEMENT

I would like to thank two people with regards to this assignment. Foremost is my wife Ailsa for tolerating me being involved with a women's rugby team in Brisbane for a year and running around the continent over two years with the Queensland women's team. Ailsa has witnessed my journey, enjoyed watching their games, met with and made lifelong friends from amongst their ranks.

Secondly to my son Norman for the hours of his time in the compilation of this edition of a special sporting team.

INTRODUCTION

They came from a diversity of fields and positions which included customs, prison officer, lawyer, childcare director, Queensland Police, wholesale nursery, copywriter, secretary, human movements student, public servant, sport and recreational officer, Airforce, process worker, student teacher, Australia Post, physiotherapist, entomologist, agricultural science, nurse, landscaping, horticulture, golf pro shop, nutritionist, council worker and a variety of other professions.

Regardless of their social standing they were obsessed with a common cause; to exceed in a team sport where all were on the same level and success would be only forthcoming on a reliance of their fellow team members.

Social standing did not exist and if I may be permitted to use the old cliché 'All for One and One for All' was the theme they pursued this obsession with. In blending together they became extremely dominant on Australian interstate level and through continued supreme performances, defeated a visiting International team ranked #2 in the world.

Following the first two years they could field an International team within themselves having fifteen players representing Australia. Such was their dominance they could fill an International pack and seven International backs. Their outstanding scoring feats and results may never be equalled at provincial level again.

This was the Queensland Women's Rugby team, 1996 to 1997.

*Above: Queensland making their way onto the pitch after their
pre-game warm up for the first ever clash against New South Wales.*

*Front Row: (L-R) Selena Worsley, Lisa Dwan, Mieke Gladwin,
Julie Anne Columbus, Shirley Russell, Vanessa Nootedoom.*

*

CONTENTS

PART I
Queensland Women 1996

Queensland Womens' Rugby
Inaugural Team - 1996

FRONT ROW (L-R): Jenny Birckel (Physio), Florrie King,
Natalie Wanrooy, Tasi Woodard (Coach), Bronwyn Calvert (Captain),
Denise Ututaonga-Scott, Christine Gold (Manager)

SECOND ROW (L-R): Jenny Beard, Vanessa Nootedoom,
Jane Hamilton, Lisa Dwan,

Mieke Gladwin, Bronwyn Laidlaw, Deena Aitken,
Maryanne Kearney, Julie Anne Columbus

THIRD ROW (L-R): Tanya Osbourne, Cathy Boulton,
Lee Anne Wilkes, Moana O'Rourke,

Karen Bucholz, Selena Worsley, Louise Jones, Shirley Russell, Perise Ili

INSERTS: Bronwyn Hart, Pearl Palaialii.

*

1: Background

In 1996 I was requested to Ballymore by the then Queensland Director of Coaching, Duncan Hall. Duncan explained to me that the then Australian Rugby Football Union (ARFU) had directed all Australian States and Territories to raise a women's representative team to later that year contest an interstate carnival to be held in Sydney. This was an initiation to finally select an Australian team to participate in the third Women's Rugby World Cup to be held in Amsterdam, Holland.

To date there had been two Women's Rugby World Cups without Australian participation.

Duncan offered me total Queensland Rugby Union (QRU) support along with the support of the Queensland Academy of Sport (QAS). He also authorised me to be a selector and to choose two other selectors to assist me in that capacity. Duncan explained that he could not release any Queensland coaching staff full time to this concept and he felt that I was the best coach in Queensland currently not affiliated with a Brisbane club. He also offered me a three-year term of coaching this team if I was willing to participate at this level.

So, on a handshake and being retired I accepted this challenge.

Being a Director of Coaching with Southern District RUFC in the early eighties I knew Duncan as a University, Queensland and Australian lock and No8.

* * *

2: Selecting a Squad

In the Brisbane Women's Rugby Club competition, the prominent team, which were unbeaten in grand finals in the short history of the Brisbane competition was the University of Queensland team. My first obligation was to observe this outstanding team while not ignoring other clubs. The only other Brisbane team that could compete with the University team was Souths Maggies (Souths play in black and white and their club is called the Magpies).

At the time not knowing the strengths of other club teams in Australia my impressions of the University of Queensland team was that surely, they would be up with the best sides in Australia.

I had a premonition that the Queensland representative squad will be built around the University and Souths Maggies teams.

I invited two other selectors in Steven Edwards (Brothers Rugby) and Margariete Howard a part time University of Queensland coach. Margariete Howard was not the 'University' Women's coach however opted to participate in their structure when it suited her. When I told the QRU management that I had invited her to be a selector and assistant coach I was looked at in a blank expression and was asked, *"Do you really want to do that?"*

With her rugby background and participation in club organisation and thinking the state team would be built around the University team I believed she would be a huge factor in my integration with the University players.

The QRU management told me, *"If that's what I wanted, so be it".*

I did not really know Margariete but knew of her background; wife of Jake Howard, current University Club President, ex-Queensland and Wallaby prop and assistant Wallaby coach, mother of Pat Howard, former Wallaby five-eight and daughter of Cyril Towers ex-Wallaby captain (1937).

Following initial state training I was, for the benefit of team harmony, forced to make Margariete be released from participation within the program. Events leading up to this release will be explained in a later segment.

*　　*　　*

As the competition season progressed, we felt we had put together a team which was worthy of state representation.

As anticipated out of the squad of twenty-four players, ten were members from the University of Queensland, eight players were from Souths Maggies, two each from the North Barbarians and Brothers clubs, one from GPS and one from Sunnybank.

*　　*　　*

The Inaugural Squad of 1996:

Ten members from the 'University of Queensland Rugby Union Club' were selected for the inaugural State side.

Back Row (L-R): Bronwyn Laidlaw, Maryanne Kearney, Deena Aitken, Mieke Gladwin, Jenny Baird

Front Row (L-R): Cathy Boulton, Natalie Wanrooy, Perise Ili, Karen Bucholz,

Lee Anne Wilkes.

Six of these members in Laidlaw, Aitken, Gladwin, Boulton, Ili and Bucholz would go on to represent Australia.

Eight members from the 'Southern Districts Rugby Union' Club were selected for the inaugural State side.

Back Row (L-R): Lisa Dwan, Bronwyn Hart, Selena Worsley, Moana O'Rourke

Front Row (L-R): Pearl Palaialii, Bronwyn Calvert, Tanya Osbourne, Shirley Russell.

Seven of these members in Dwan, Hart, Worsley, Palaialii, Calvert, Osbourne and Russell would go on to represent Australia.

Two members from the 'Norths Barbarians Rugby Club' were selected for the inaugural State side. Jane Hamilton (left) and Julie Anne Columbus. Both represented Australia in 1995.

Right: Two members from the 'Brothers Rugby Club' were selected for the inaugural State side. Louise Jones (left) and Florrie King.

Left: Vanessa Nootedoom was selected from the 'GPS Rugby Club' for the inaugural State side. Vanessa was originally selected from the Townsville (North Queensland) rugby union area and went on to represent Australia.

Centre: Denise Ututaonga-Scott was selected from the 'Sunnybank Rugby Union Club'.

Right: Bronwyn Calvert was the inaugural Queensland Team Captain. Bronwyn was a Captain and Centre from the 'Souths Maggies' rugby team.

* * *

3: First Meeting

Our first team meeting was held in the referee's club at Ballymore where first introductions, training and playing philosophies were explained.

I am a defensive coach, my philosophy being that if a team cannot score against you, they will not beat you (I started captain/coaching at the age of twenty-five and my philosophy and attitude to coaching in that respect has never changed). Defensive rugby has to be taught on blackboard and unit drills whereas attacking rugby is a natural instinct requiring support, continuity and attacking the opposition's weakest areas.

I broke the team up into 'Units', being;

- Unit 1: The 'tight five'
- Unit 2: The backrowers
- Unit 3: Halfback to outside centres
- Unit 4: The three fullbacks, being; the primary, right and left fullbacks.

At all warm up sessions with ball involvement these units were to run separately within their units thereby getting to know one another and learning of each individual's weaknesses and strengths.

Blackboard lessons on each units' responsibilities both in offence and defence were outlined.

Each unit has entirely different functions in rugby however in game situations, they fit together like a jigsaw puzzle and the team can always set up three and at times four effective lines of defence. These lines of defence are also very advantageous in the case of immediate turnovers, where the team now has depth in support and attack.

The individual units could see the overall effectiveness of this aspect of team organisation and certainly it appeared to them that although each unit did have different functions it was plain to them how effective it was in supporting, not only the individual but other units and the team. Playing field running in game situations would clear up any doubts about effectiveness in defence.

I attended the first national coaching course held in Queensland in the mid-seventies under the new ARFU system run by the appointment of a National Coaching Director. One of the first indoctrinations I absorbed from this course that stuck in my mind for the rest of my coaching career was the introduction of the four team principles I always based my coaching around, being;

1: Go Forward

2: Support

3: Continuity

4: Pressure

These principles were drummed into this squad, however first things first. To win a game of rugby a team first must have physical domination. This physical domination is initiated with the first scrum.

At the conclusion of this meeting, I announced the team's captain in Bronwyn Calvert. The reason for her nomination was firstly being Souths Maggies' captain and as explained in Part III Chapter 3 of this book 'The Brisbane Scene'.

I had to confide in Bronwyn seeking complexities about

women in sport in this case rugby, as I've never been involved with women in any sport and I was confronted with a lot of 'unknowns.' Bronwyn was straight forward with me and an understanding was initiated. She did clear up a lot of 'mysteries' for me and she became a person I could turn to in seeking little oddities with women and a relationship was formed which carried over to state level. Bronwyn was of a great assistance to me in such matters. Bronwyn's occupation was a nutritionist and was known to talk to classes and in public meetings. She could address groups being another point in her favour for the captaincy ... an extremely competent individual.

* * *

4: The Scrum

For those who have played rugby and been a member of a scrum know only too well the implications of a sound scrum. Knowing all individuals possess different heights (and limbs) weights and skills, one cannot provide an effective scrum overnight as it takes hours, days, weeks and months to provide something near perfection. This Queensland team had not only athleticism but size and power in their forwards and I knew that this scrum would be the initiation of Queensland success.

For the first weeks of training the squad was split up, backs trained on Ballymore #3 and the forwards on Ballymore's #2 field with a scrum machine presence. Each forward was individually introduced to the scrum machine taking in all the key factors to successful scrummaging including body mechanics functions. The frontrowers were eventually introduced as a unit then the locks. When the tight five became an effective unit, the backrowers were engaged in wedging the front row and the #8 locking the two locks. Rotation of all forwards was not overlooked to assist also in the best combinations. Coordination in 'snap shoving' and 'straight leg lock' (stability), on ball presentation, ball feedback and channelling from the scrum was layered into the learning. For the first weeks the forwards just packed hundreds of scrums, checking and adjusting body mechanics, grips and other associated small functions in making a more powerful scrummaging unit.

The better they became the more they wanted to perfect it.

Other forwards told me how the front rowers shoulders had in some cases become red raw, bruised and sore with constant scrum machine engagement on the pads although not one player complained to me about it. They understood that this was where physical domination was initiated.

I wish to express my gratitude to Des Kissane, a QRU coach who was lent to us to run and assist in all factors of individual and unit scrummaging. I don't know if Des was ever told, however 'Ugly Day' games were played for 'The Des Kissane Cup' in both Sydney 1996 and Adelaide 1997 ... see 'Lighter Times on Tour'.

* * *

*Left: Queensland and Australian Props in Julie Anne Columbus (left)
and Pearl Palaialii.*

*Queensland Locks/Second Rowers, Lisa Dwan from 'Queensland Police
Academy' (centre) and Mieke Gladwin of 'Queensland University
Rugby' were to become Australia's Lock pairing.*

5: The Backs

During the forwards scrum machine isolation, the backs we're not idle concentrating on ball skills, supporting play, individual skills, switch passing, side stepping, swerving, tackling and above all making all fullbacks (Unit 4) competent in fullback play. Fortunately, we had a primary fullback, Maryanne Kearney and two other competent players in that position Bronwyn Laidlaw (centre/fullback) and Denise Ututaonga-Scott (winger/fullback). Whilst another winger in Jenny Beard learnt that positional play on a rotation basis so during games a fullback would be inserting themselves into backlines (Unit 3) on all occasions (positional duplication) creating overlaps.

Individual skills weaknesses where acknowledged and practised on while maintaining strengths, not only improving individuals but also improving the team by eliminating those weaknesses.

Fitness levels were raised with the emphasis on the reorganisation of quick realignments to attack on the opposite side of the field continuously changing open sides. The construction of two backlines was implemented with emphasis placed on duplicating oneself in the same movement. Their willingness to improve was obvious and I could sense they believed great rewards was forthcoming.

Visits to the Queensland Academy of Sports (QAS) was beneficial with emphasis on strength training not only for the body but also the arms. It became noticeable over time that while their ball passing accuracy did not deteriorate their passing range increased significantly leading to a more expansive game.

After several weeks had elapsed it was time for the forwards and backs to come together for unit and team coordination.

Above: Halves. (L-R): Perise Ili, Florrie King,
Karen Bucholz and Vanessa Nootedoom.

Ili, Bucholz and Nootedoom went onto Australian representative honours.

Above: Wingers and Fullbacks. (L-R): Denise Ututaonga-Scott, Jenny Beard, Maryanne Kearney and Bronwyn Laidlaw.

*　　*　　*

6: The First Union

The first session with team coordination the backs were brought over from Ballymore #3 to be united with their forward team members. The very first drill carried out was to pack as many backs as possible onto the scrum machine platform. A scrum was packed on the machine and with a 'snap shove' on ball entry followed by the continued forward momentum. Here was a scrum machine been propelled 20-30 metres over Ballymore #2 with a squad of backs on the machine with exclamations, *'OMG ... Holy Shit ... How good is this?'*

One could observe these backs had never experienced such forward power and drive. One could also observe the backs eyes light up and some were heard to state, *'How good is it to be playing behind this pack?'* One could not help but notice the confidence of the backs had been elevated and the keenness was obvious among them to begin team training while the forwards wanted to keep showing off on the scrum machine.

I had previously stated I had in my possession an extremely big, athletic pack of forwards, who not only were aware of their potential but now hungry for improvement and success. With the forwards knowing the capabilities of the backs through club rugby, we now had a set of backs and forwards with mutual admiration for each other and fully knew they could ably complement each other in a game situation.

*   *   *

7: Possession Time – No Kick Zones

Heard from an opposition player...
"To score against Queensland, firstly you have to get the ball off them."

A game of rugby is played for 80 minutes and usually you would expect teams to have equal possession for 40 minutes each. If we could steal five minutes of opposition time it comes down to a 45-35 minutes of possession there by limiting the opposition time for scoring opportunities and lengthening ours.

Most rugby players do not possess kicking skills especially tactical kicking which takes a long time and continual practice to master also in conjunction with support players. We did not have that time to dedicate to this skill so in our situation we developed 'no kick zones'.

If a penalty was awarded to us, centre field, it was always a tap taken by the 'tight five' forwards (Unit 1) and they run the ball up field always to the right-hand side of the ground. When met by the opposition and forward momentum ceased, they would set up a maul allowing Units 3 and 4 to have a full width of the pitch to operate in (expansive rugby). Their support in depth or in case of a breakdown in momentum was by Unit 2 to ensure continuity. By having 'no kick zones' we were retaining possession for longer periods. Kicking the ball once in the opposition half was absolutely taboo as ball retention was our highest priority.

Now let's think of 'stealing' ten minutes of opposition time. In possession it now becomes a 50-30-minute imbalance.

Team principle #4 is 'Pressure' and when applied in defence opposition teams out of frustration of failing to advance the ball to the gain line and going backwards in possession had only one alternative, which was to kick it thereby presenting us with their time. As games in the future progressed this team became very obsessed with starving opposition of possession, while they had the ability overall in using their possession time to great effect.

Note: Overheard at a later function;

"To score against Queensland, firstly you have to get the ball off them."

I believe the points for and against following the first Australian Women's Rugby Championships can justify the Queensland team's domination.

Another skill we worked on was protecting oneself as a ball carrier. The simple mechanic was to turn side on to the tackler just before impact offering hip and shoulder to the defender while keeping forward drive into the tackler with intent, *"If you are going to tackle me it's going to hurt you"*. This action also moves the ball away from the opposition for their own support player or setting up a maul ripping platform if forward momentum ceased. After all ball protection was a primary issue, denying opposition the ball and keeping them on a starvation diet of possession was vital.

Two of our forwards in Bronwyn Hart and Pearl Palaialii became exceedingly skilful in this art and on many occasions left a would-be tackler prone on the ground without losing forward momentum. These two players a prop and hooker, both compact, fast and exceedingly aggressive were two thirds of a club (Souths Maggies) and to become the future Queensland and Australian front row.

Over a short space of time all our forwards became skilful in the art of body mechanics pertaining to ball carrying into opposition defence knowing instant support was available to ensure continuity of play. The backs not to be denied were also skilled in the art of setting up a maul platform if unfortunate enough to be apprehended as a ball carrier. I think in some games a 50-30-minute possession was excelled.

A compact, strong and aggressive Queensland (to become Australian) front row in Julie Anne Columbus, Pearl Palaialii and hooker Bronwyn Hart, ably supported by frontrowers Lee Anne Wilkes, Louise Jones and Moana O'Rourke dominated Australian interstate rugby.

*   *   *

8: Intensifying the Training

Training now at team level became more intense with both forwards and backs complementing each other in general play.

Often #1 and #2 Units would play in a game situation against Units 3 and 4 from line out and scrum situations, which was invaluable especially for Unit 2. With Units 3 and 4 winning the line outs and scrums it magnified Unit 2's defensive obligations and anticipation of what Units 3 and 4 could produce to beat their defensive skills. During this time Unit 1 was deploying for the next phase of play.

I would have sessions where Units 1 and 3 would play against Units 2 and 4 in both attack and defensive plays. This training also gave the three fullbacks rotation and development of their coordination skills. I may add we were fortunate in having two of the best fullbacks in the country with one a more than capable centre/ wing in Bronwyn Laidlaw, who in

Maryanne Kearney from 'University of Queensland.'

coming years represented Queensland and Australia in all three positions such was the versatility of her ability.

The other full back was Maryanne Kearney, the most underrated fullback in Australia whose last line defence was unmatched at national level. Both players were from the University of Queensland Club.

Finally, such was the coordination of all four units that no matter when a breakdown of play occurred, they instantly knew what their next phase would be at all times being positionally situated to carry out that phase.

As training continued over the weeks, I could notice that the players had huge confidence in their fellow team mates no matter what the rotation of squad members outside the fifteen, other members would act as opposition and the contests were fierce with this training always being carried out under game situations.

*   *   *

9: Scrum Domination

At a time of night training the QRU's Under 18s (male) were training at Ballymore and as I knew both coaches, I requested them to give us some live scrummaging as it would benefit both squads. Even though training had been intense as at this time we still had not experienced any live scrummaging. The Under 18s coach consented. One must realise that the Queensland State Under 18s are quite a large unit and I remember quoting their forwards were almost as big as our A grade forwards in the 1960s. Following three scrums the under 18s coach said, "No more scrums" as the women's squad had utterly decimated them on all occasions and I know it had humiliated them. The coach said to me later that their squad had only come together and no time had been allocated to that set play.

I did organise a game against the Queensland XXXX (Fourex) Golden Oldies team whose home ground and clubhouse is at Ballymore. The XXXX Goldies even though in their late 30s, 40s, 50s and 60s were of some note being ex-State and ex-A Grade players.

An enjoyable and very even game was had by all followed by a barbecue and drinks sponsored by the XXXX Team.

* * *

10: The Test

At our last training night following a light team run it was back to the scrum machine for our forwards where the scrum was to be assessed by Alec Evans, the Queensland and Wallabies 'scrum doctor'.

Upon setting the first scrum Alec inspected the grippage, studdage, feet placement, compactness and body mechanics. He moved to the side of the scrum and tried to move it by vigorously pushing and pulling it ... the pack never moved. (It is a fact that if grips, studdage and mechanics are correct, to move one you must move the whole pack).

Alec then set a second scrum and attempted to move the scrum from the other side ... the scrum never moved. We rotated all the forwards in the scrum and then had scrums with ball entry, channelling the ball through channels 1, 2 and 3.

Finally, after very close examinations of all individuals and team scrums Alec stood the scrum up and stated, *"Congratulations. I have nothing to offer here."*

For scrummaging we had passed the most stringent test in Australian rugby.

* * *

11: First Game

"In the first scrum when we drove the Alberta pack back on their ball input and continued their backward progress and won their scrum, the sensation was that great, I almost had an orgasm."

* * *

Prior to Australia's first Women's Interstate carnival, we in Queensland had no idea of our status, how good we were or otherwise. However, we were fortunate to test ourselves against a Canadian touring team compiled by players from Alberta, one of the primary rugby provinces of Canada (the other being British Columbia).

Most of their players had attended the first two Women's Rugby World Cup representing Canada so we knew we were up against a seasoned team which is what we wanted.

Canada along with New Zealand, the USA, the UK, France and a host of European nations have been playing international rugby for some twelve years and had attended the first two Women's Rugby World Cups. Whereas Australia had been left behind and even now was only entering its fourth year of rugby. From what data we could gather on the Alberta team we found they were one of the top provincial teams in Canada and worthy of Canadian representation.

The Queensland squad had twelve days and six training sessions left to play their first match against Alberta on

Queensland's international rugby venue, Ballymore. We knew we had a lot more work to do so I allocated a full squad training six-hour day on Saturday the 22nd of June at Ballymore. Along with Des Kissane from the QRU coaching staff for the first two hours the forwards again were subjected to power scrummaging on the scrum machine to obtain the standard of perfection I was seeking.

The Alberta team had begun their Australian tour with a game against New South Wales and as news of the game filtered through, Alberta's strength lay in their scrummaging and forward strength virtually nullifying New South Wales' forwards and dominating them in all forward contests.

Alberta's second match was against the ACT and once again we learned that the ACT did not win one of their own scrums and only one line out. My emphasis on scrummaging was vindicated. So well had our scrum advanced I couldn't believe that any provincial team could be superior in this area. The Queensland scrum as previously stated were big, powerful and athletic. I have put so much in writing on scrum emphasis however I must state that never had our lineout training been neglected. We had two locks in Mieke Gladwin and Lisa Dwan who were both outstanding line out specialists and in an earlier prediction prior to our first Interstate National Championships I predicted that Mieke Gladwin would be Australia's primary and best lock in the country. Mieke was a University of Queensland lock and with her second-row partner Lisa Dwan (Souths Maggie's) both represented Australia at international level.

So impressed was I with their scrum, I with them decided to use this strength as a truly attacking weapon. If the New South Wales and ACT had been demolished by Alberta in the scrum area, they in turn would naturally expect that the Queensland pack would be similar in standard. On our last training session, match eve, I outlined my belief in the standard the scrum had achieved and explained we should attack their scrum from the very first scrum of the game. The forwards took this in and such was the belief in themselves in this area one said, "Yeah! Let's do it!" followed by all others eagerly supporting the concept. I knew if our pack could nullify the opposition in their power area it would be a setback they would never recover from. I also believed our backs were capable of putting the 'icing on the cake' such was their precision and pace.

Here we were at Ballymore on the 24th of June at approximately 8:00 PM with eleven backs standing on a scrum machine platform with brakes partially applied and eight forwards powering the machine along. Once again, the backs were quite astonished at this little exhibition of power scrummaging.

*   *   *

I thought a little motto was needed so a piece I drew up for the next three years were the last words spoken before running onto the rugby pitch and recited by all:

"We are Queensland
We are history
We are family
We are as one
We are Queensland
I am Queensland"

*   *   *

"*In the first scrum when we drove the Alberta pack back on their ball input and continued their backward progress and won their scrum, the sensation was that great I almost had an orgasm.*" One of my forwards relating to me on our success over Alberta in power scrummaging ... speaker's name withheld.

The team, the first to be adorned in maroon representing Queensland looked absolutely magnificent. One could notice great pride emanating from these individuals in which I could relate to, the same pride I had for them collectively. I sensed that they were never going to let this great rugby state down.

An unexpected crowd had arrived at Ballymore to view this history making spectacle perhaps out of curiosity more than any other reason. I noticed a large group of that supporter base was from the women of the eight rugby clubs in Brisbane along with friends, family, husbands and boyfriends of the players themselves. It was pleasant to notice that some QRU officials were in attendance. None of those present at the game left disappointed at this first exposure to women's rugby at provincial level, such was the intensity, speed and coordination of the backs/forwards complementing each other in their unit skills responsibilities. A wonderful spectacle of a hard-uncompromising forwards clash, complemented by a backline with speed and a skills level that would do justice to any team on any level.

For weeks following the game, men in rugby who witnessed the game spoke of the unbelievable skills level in women's rugby. I could relate to their amazement as I also in January, had been confronted with and taken aback when first being exposed to these dedicated athletes and the natural ability they possessed.

I believe that after the third scrum of the day in the first ten minutes, Alberta realised that huge asset they had over

Australian teams to date was nullified and they were going to endure a long afternoon. The Queensland forwards paved the way for the first two tries of the game scored by winger Cathy Boulton following a wonderful display of supporting rugby by the backs and the second by captain and centre Bronwyn Calvert, her second possession of the ball in the movement. Power prop Pearl Palaialii scored a third from continuity in forward play. Centre Tanya Osbourne converted the try and Alberta kicked a penalty goal to produce a half time score; Queensland 17 Alberta 3.

Cathy Boulton became the first player to score a try in Queensland Women's Rugby. Cathy through 1996/1997 scored ten tries (ten games though played in eight) before going away to the 1998 'National Championships' in Darwin. I have no doubt she would have scored further tries and may still be the highest try scorer representing Queensland in Women's Rugby.

It may be noted that Cathy Boulton became the first women's

player to score a try in Queensland Rugby and Pearl Palaialii the first forward to try.

Queensland continued the second half assault with fullback Maryanne Kearney's insertion into the backline, producing perhaps the most perfect piece of set play of the game to score between the posts. This try was followed by hooker Bronwyn Hart and No8 Deena Aitken five pointers with replacement half Florrie King touching down following a huge forward surge initiated from a twenty-metre lineout, which took play to within one metre from the Alberta goal line. Tanya Osbourne converted two tries with the final score being Queensland 41 Alberta 3.

*   *   *

Carolyn Warren from North Queensland refereed Queensland's first game and received huge accolades from the QRU for her control of the match.

Queensland 41 – Alberta 3

Scorers — Queensland: C. Boulton, B. Calvert, P. Palaialii, M. Kearney, B. Hart, D. Aitken, F. King - Tries (Tries 7)

T. Osbourne — Conversions 3

Scorers - Alberta: L. Evenson — Penalty Goal

Referee: Carolyn Warren (North Queensland)

*　　*　　*

This game had done more to lift the profile of women's rugby in this state than any other occasion to date. Disappointingly so, was the lack of media coverage to this historic sporting occasion where the game received scant coverage (scores only) by the *Courier Mail*.

At the 'After Game Function' from the Alberta management:

"How many Queenslanders are selected in the Australian President's XV for our last match on tour?"

"Eleven ... Eight forwards"

"Oh my God!" was the reaction of an Alberta player.

Forwards: (No8) Deena Aitken, (Frontrowers) Julie Anne Columbus, Bronwyn Hart, Pearl Palaialii, Lee Anne Wilkes, (Lock) Lisa Dwan, (Backrowers) Shirley Russell and Selena Worsley.

Backs: (Centres) Bronwyn Calvert and Tanya Osbourne, (Winger) Kathy Boulton.

The Australian President's XV, captained by Brisbane Barbarians Julie Anne Columbus defeated Alberta in a very entertaining match 32-0. Two players that really stood out were ACT's winger Sharon O'Kane playing in only her fourth rugby match, scoring three tries all with pace and deception and Northern Territory's fullback Naomi Roberts who had a marvellous game in counter attack setting up scoring opportunities and scoring a try herself.

At the Queensland Rugby Union AGM on Wednesday the 26th of June 1996 a prominent member of the QRU confronted me and stated, *"Congratulations Tasi, that was a magnificent game of rugby Saturday (Queensland versus Alberta). More pleasant to watch than many A Grade matches because of the ball movement in comparison to the kicking option. In fact, the female referee (Carolyn Warren) had an outstanding game, also a better performance than many of her counterparts are capable of controlling."*

This was one of the numerous compliments I received over the following weeks, which I in turn passed onto the players, deservingly they had earned for their dedication and hard work to achieve this result.

12: A Slight Implosion
– Parting of the Ways

Following a team meeting in the referees' room I was still inside when from outside a commotion erupted, loud shouting and a dressing down was in progress. On moving outside unfortunately it was Margariete Howard verbally giving Vanessa Nootedoom (the five-eighth brought down from Townsville) telling her, *"You'll never be a five-eighth, move to another position, anywhere, even back to Townsville. You will never play in my team."*

I quickly intervened immediately stopped the onset and told Margariete, *"This player was brought down from Townsville to play five-eighth and that's where she will play"*, and dispersed the team gathering.

Vanessa was obviously very upset, being belittled in front of the team members and crying following the haranguing she had just received. I consoled her and told her to dismiss the incident. The primary five-eighth in the squad was Perise Ili an outstanding 'University of Queensland' player, who would be the primary five-eighth no question about that.

This incident played on my mind as disruption within the team was the last element, I needed seeing to date the squad was running on a high.

*   *   *

Margariete Howard was not the University's women's coach, however, would takeover coaching the team when it suited her; I may digress here.

At a much later date while at the University clubhouse following a game, I questioned a University's coach, "*In what capacity did Margariete have within the club as a coach?*"

He replied, "*None. However, when it suited her, she will present herself for a coaching session with any University team as long as it was a team high on the competition ladder.*"

He followed by saying, "*She would have nothing to do with a team that was not performing well in the competition.*"

I then asked, "*Why would team coaches tolerate this?*"

He explained, "*It was out of respect for her husband Jake, the University club president, ex-Queensland and Wallaby prop and past assistant coach with the Wallabies.*

*   *   *

I spoke with several senior women squad members, who were not University members, on the aspect of being coached under her, keeping in mind for the first weeks I was heavily involved with the forwards while Margariete mainly controlled the running of the backs. I did this following a training schedule implemented by me, they replied and were adamant that although the subject was never spoken of, the feeling was that as they didn't play for University and had not been coached by her then they didn't really know how to play rugby as she constantly faulted the non-University players during sessions.

It was slowly dawning on me why QRU staff questioned my

earlier decision to have Margariete Howard as a selector and on my coaching staff.

I mulled over the situation and realised I could not possibly have disruption within the squad and to remove one member would solve the growing problem.

At the next training session, I bought together the squad sat them on the ground and personally thanked Margariete for her valuable input into the initiation of raising and assisted training of the team. I then added that this training session would be the last one with Margariete's attendance and once again thanked her on behalf of the team and the QRU.

Margariete's response was, *"I will never speak to you again"* and departed.

Some University players after Margariete's departure just patted me on the back and nodded. As I became more conversant with University players some had confided in me that at times at club level their training has been disrupted by Margariete's insistence of taking the training session.

With training in harmony and back on track and after an in-depth analysis of the Alberta game and acknowledging our deficiencies, we set out to rectify those problems and prepare ourselves for the upcoming National Championships in Sydney.

*   *   *

13: Golden Goldie

It would be remiss of me not to mention the outstanding work of our most competent manager in Christine Gold (Goldie). Managers are often overlooked when speaking of team successes however a good manager does all behind the scenes hard work and a competent manager allows players to concentrate on their playing responsibilities while the manager attends to all administrative matters. In this capacity Goldie was outstanding. Moving a rugby team around the country is no small task. On the Queensland team initiation at our first meeting a training agenda was laid out. The first item on training nights was allocated to Goldie to keep all players informed on administrative matters taking questions and attending to any individuals concerns.

I learnt from my army experience in keeping the troops informed with clarity in communication being a prime asset also keeping harmony in a unit .

Goldie would implore players, "Any problems please come and see me." No issue was beyond her capacity and her work in conjunction with the QRU was beyond reproach. I was fortunate to have Goldie in this capacity such was her efficiency and I requested her availability for future years. Her work was as important as any player and never once did I have a player approach me over an administration problem. Thanks Goldie.

*   *   *

14: The First Interstate Series

1996 was the first year that a truly Interstate series was played with teams representing the ACT, New South Wales, Northern Territory, Queensland, South Australia, Victoria and Western Australia.

In previous years this National Championship series was played between the ACT, Northern Territory and club teams from Sydney, Brisbane and regional areas. In 1995 the Northern Territory defeated a club team from Brisbane, Souths 5-0 in the final of the National Championship to earn the title of 'National Champions', however 1996 saw the first real interstate series where all teams present were at provincial level.

The series was played over a week in Sydney between the 14th July and the 21st July with two pools formed. The draw was as follows:

Pool A:	Pool B:
New South Wales	Victoria
Western Australia	ACT
South Australia	Northern Territory
Queensland	

Note: In 1997 an eighth team was added being the 'Australian Services Rugby Union'.

The pool matches were played on Monday 15th, Wednesday 17th and Friday the 19th with finals to be played on Saturday the 20th. Teams that came third in each pool would play off teams that came second in each pool would play off with the winners of each pool to then play off for the National Championship 1996.

From this series an Australian squad of thirty members would be selected, later to be trimmed to twenty-two to play a test against New Zealand in August 1996 (New Zealand are ranked number one in the world winning the first two Women's Rugby World Cup).

In round one, Monday 15th July, New South Wales defeated South Australia 75-0 and Queensland defeated Western Australia 47-10 in Pool A, while Northern Territory defeated Victoria in a much closer result in Pool B.

In Round 2 on Wednesday 17th, New South Wales played Western Australia in the opening match of the day. I wish to talk of this match as it was quite amusing in that New South Wales after their big win over South Australia the previous round went out with the pure intention to score more points against Western Australia than what Queensland were able to. If they were able to score a bigger win the result would serve two purposes, it would give them confidence in their own capabilities and secondly, in the event of a drawn match against Queensland it will give them a huge for and against record which may result in them winning Pool A.

At the completion of the match New South Wales defeated Western Australia 49-0 much to the great jubilation within the New South Wales camp. After two matches New South Wales had a plus 87 points in their favour over Queensland.

In our meeting room at our last training session before leaving Queensland I named the first two teams to play the respective matches versing Western Australia and South Australia. We had a squad of twenty-four players and I explained that by the end of game two I wanted every player within our squad to have played a game as not only was this the National Championships but also selection for a National squad and I wanted all players to have equal exposure before the National selectors.

Both Western Australia and South Australia as with all teams were an unknown quantity, however New South Wales, the ACT and Queensland did have games against the touring Alberta (Canadian team) leading up to this Interstate series with Queensland having an outstanding result against Alberta.

Within our squad of twenty-four players there was very little difference in ability between all members in most positions, however there was a gap in experience and maturity in some players. We had selected this squad with a view to give some very young talented players exposure at this level being insurance for the future of women's rugby in Queensland.

The two teams selected to play in the first two matches of the series were blended with youth, maturity and combinations keeping in mind that eighteen members came from within the ranks of two clubs.

There was never any mention to the team to play South Australia of trying to defeat them by more than 87 points, that alone would be a huge ask, however the focus was to win well. At the completion of the match Queensland defeated South Australia 119-0. The feature of this game was that Queensland scored five tries from South Australian scrums.

New South Wales who had stayed to watch the outcome was very dejected and even then, I could sense a defeatist attitude amongst them as they trudged past. After this second match, all Queensland players had played a game with six members having played in both run on sides and some others from reserve capacity.

In between these matches the ACT comfortably defeated Victoria. I watched this match and it became apparent that the ACT was a very well drilled team even though smaller than the large Queensland forwards their mobility, tenacity and skills level was very good. I suspected they would defeat the Northern Territory comfortably to decide the winners of pool B.

On Thursday the 18th, a game free day, Julie Anne Columbus (prop) came to me prior to a two-hour rest period and told me, *"The team had made arrangements to go to the South Australian camp and assist them with scrummaging and backs training and did I mind?"*

"Of course not." The South Australian team was anxiously looking forward to the session and it gave the Queensland team huge credibility amongst other teams.

On Friday the 19th of July, round three matches, I said, *"With due respect to the other teams, today was to be crunch day as the best four teams in the championship were to play off to be their respective pool winners; New South Wales versus Queensland and the ACT versus Northern Territory."*

Western Australia defeated South Australia in the opening match and the ACT justified my belief in them by outclassing Northern Territory with a runaway result in the second half. The Northern Territories claim as National Champions, a 'clayton's claim' was over. In fact, I firmly believe that the top two club teams in Brisbane, premiers University of Queensland and Souths Maggies would be superior teams to them.

Prior to the New South Wales versus Queensland match during our teams warm up a reporter from one of the Sydney papers came over and introduced himself. He said to me, *"Tasi I have just come from the New South Wales pre-game gathering and it is complete chaos over there, everyone is talking and yelling with nothing constructive being done."* Then said, *"There is no control it's a shamble."* He added, *"I have been watching on for some time the Queensland's pre-game drills, nothing is being said, they all seem focused, the contrast is unbelievable."*

A large crowd had gathered to watch the New South Wales versus Queensland clash and to my surprise, with the exception of a small group, support for the Queensland team was overwhelming.

This I put down to the coaching and management staff of the New South Wales team which portrayed a team arrogance in that they would not welcome an opposing team onto the field nor would they clap a team off the field at the conclusion of match. This not only illustrates a show of arrogance but also bad sportsmanship. This *'we are better than you'* attitude does not go down well with the sporting public. I do not blame their players as they only do what they are told. In contrast I always insist on my team to clap opposition teams on and off the field regardless of the result. For this game New South Wales ran onto the field first and straight to their positions for the kick off. I told the Queensland team to run on and line up on the centre line. The New South Wales team looked at each other waiting for a reaction. Then very reluctantly and spasmodically some walked up to the Queensland team followed by others and shook hands, although it appeared unwillingly.

This Queensland team with the exception of two injuries was the team that comprehensively defeated Alberta and this team was a big, athletic team and quite intimidating when standing opposite another team. This display in lining up on the centre line served two purposes, sportsmanship and intimidation.

*   *   *

I may digress here and speak briefly on the fourth team principle 'pressure'. We practiced constantly on the 'pressure principle' not in attack, which comes naturally with ball in hand but in defence. This comes with fitness but is practiced to get to the gain line in defence before the opposition can get to the gain line with ball in hand. With the opposition in ball possession, constantly going backwards they would end up kicking it in frustration, 'thank you for possession'. Counter attack from opposition frustration was a Queensland hallmark.

*   *   *

Prior to the New South Wales match I had noted their five-eighth was a good player, however quite petite in comparison to our North Queensland five-eighth Vanessa Nootedoom, big, fast, strong and an immensely powerful runner. I selected Vanessa to play this match under the instruction that if we were in the New South Wales twenty-five and she received the ball from set or phase play, she was to run at her opposite number no evasion or passing the ball but to run straight over the top of her.

This game was totally dominated by Queensland with New South Wales getting into the Queensland half only on one occasion in the first half and only four times in the second half. Such was the superiority that late in the game camped in the New South Wales half with them in possession they could only resort to kicking the ball in frustration, in attempting to run the ball they were simply cut down on their own side of the gain line.

Queensland scored two tries in the first half, the first by

Queensland's and Australia's most dynamic backrow forward in Selena Worsley from an intercept and the second by Natalie Wanrooy a small, however tenacious breakaway through a constant forward build up.

Queensland scored another two tries in the second half. One by Vanessa Nootedoom who when receiving a ball from our own maul in the New South Wales twenty-five ran straight over the top of New South Wales five-eighth and even after Vanessa had scored the try the poor trampled five-eighth was still attempting to get off the ground. If I could make a comparison, those who witnessed through a thousand replays of the great Jonah Lomu running over the top of the England fullback in a World Cup match, believe me was a like situation. Queensland scored another try by the very versatile Bronwyn Laidlaw, who ended up playing fullback, centre and wing for both Queensland and Australia. Scoring two tries in each half, with one conversion and a penalty goal resulted in a 25-0 win.

At the completion of the game the Queensland team formed up on the sideline as with our usual practice, clapped the New South Wales team from the field, whom I might add were quite surprised at this little display. In a huddle their team had a brief chat and reciprocated. I only hoped the coaching and management staff of New South Wales would change their attitude. To New South Wales I'm sure it embarrassed some of their players, however all New South Wales teams and I have experienced playing against them for six years on different levels, have an attitude of superiority and *'born to rule'*.

For the finals on Saturday the 20th, winners of Pool A Queensland would play the winners of Pool B the ACT for the National crown with New South Wales versing Northern

Left: Karen Bucholz was 'University of Queensland's' exceptional Halfback, who in defence played a Breakaway's role. Her defence for size was outstanding, which led her to Queensland and Australian representative honours.

Right: The four best Centres in Australia in my opinion. (L-R): Bronwyn Calvert and Tanya Osbourne (Souths Centres), Cathy Boulton and Bronwyn Laidlaw (University Centres). All four represented Australia. I believed that Tanya Osbourne was the women's equivalent to the Wallabies great Centre, Michael O'Connor.

Territory for third and fourth respectively and Western Australia to play Victoria for fifth and sixth.

Victoria surprisingly defeated Western Australia and New South Wales easily accounted for the Territorians.

After lunch on Friday the 19th I requested our four centres, the pairing of University of Queensland centres Bronwyn Laidlaw and Cathy Boulton and Souths Maggies centres in Bronwyn Calvert and Tanya Osbourne along with five-eighth Perise Ili for a meeting. We sat down and I explained that the reason for first calling Perise Ili to the meeting was I believed she was not playing up to expectations whereas Vanessa Nootedoom was playing the 'house down' and I was at a quandary who to select for the final. The finals team would be selected and announced on Saturday morning and prior to a training run before the final. Perise left the meeting.

Perise was always the primary five-eighth in the squad and along with our halfback in Karen Bucholz also the University of Queensland half, had played for several years as the University's halves and did have an outstanding combination. At club level in being reigning premiers and never beaten in grand finals it was hard to ignore the pairing.

Back to the centres. In my opinion they were the best four centres in Australia and to leave any out was a loss of talent. I explained that as I intended to play all four centres, however two would be wingers as any of the four were superior to our touring wingers. I put it to them for their opinion on this very, however fortunate problem. After discussion the four centres agreed that the selection was in my hands and they would be happy with my final decision. I contemplated on this selection for some time, however I did believe that Tanya Osbourne was the best outside centre in Australia so she was to play in that position. Her club centre in Bronwyn Calvert would play inside her as I did not want to split combinations. If I could make a comparison, Tanya Osbourne in women's rugby was akin to the great Michael O'Connor in Australian and International rugby.

Perise Ili got the nod to play five-eighth.

For the final, again Queensland surprisingly had a very supportive crowd and responded accordingly by running in three tries, all scored by Perise Ili with Cathy Boulton scoring a fourth in the first half. One conversion and a penalty goal gave Queensland a 25-0 half time lead. The ACT to their credit fought back bravely in the second half scoring a try and keeping Queensland to one try (again to five-eighth Perise Ili) for a final result Queensland 30 ACT 5.

The ACT became only the second team to score a try against Queensland during the series.

Perise Ili and I had a good player/coach relationship and I was told after the game by other players that following the after lunch chat the previous day, Perise retired to her quarters where a few tears were shed believing she had forfeited her position. However, on the morning of the final at the team announcement she was very relieved.

Even though Perise and I have never spoken of the issue, in scoring four tries in the final I have no doubt following the game she would have thought and maybe passed onto a few friends, *"Get that into you Coach"*.

Perhaps that after lunch chat was beneficial to both Perise and Queensland. As explained previously the ACT were a well drilled team. In the five matches played by Queensland in 1996, they were the only team to bring to notice some deficiencies in the Queensland side that no other team had been capable of doing. The ACT had earnt respect from Queensland and a return match hopefully in 1997 would be eagerly looked forward to.

At the completion of the 1996 National Championships Queensland had proved that the power base of women's rugby in Australia firmly lies in their State.

Captain Bronwyn Calvert accepted the huge trophy on behalf of Queensland at the presentation function that evening also learning that Queensland had twelve players named in the Australian squad of thirty.

Left: Shelley Lingman was the Northern Territory Coach and a National Selector. Shelley either had a very good team, however was a very poor Coach or was biased in selecting seven Northern Territory players in the National Squad following the '1996 National Championships'.

Unbelievably we listened as seven Northern Territory players were selected and only three from the ACT. The coach of the Northern Territory team, Shelley Lingman was also a National selector.

* * *

Standings at the completion of the 1996 National Championships:

1. Queensland
2. ACT
3. New South Wales
4. Northern Territory
5. Victoria
6. Western Australia
7. South Australia

*   *   *

Queensland's record for the four matches in the 1996 National Championship and including the Canadian (Alberta) game:

International Provincial:

Defeated Alberta (Canada) 41-3

Australian National Championships
— Sydney 14-21 July 1996

Defeated W.A. 47-10

Defeated S.A. 119-0

Defeated N.S.W. 25-0

Final: Defeated A.C.T. 30-5

Points For – 262 Points Against – 18

Tries For – 42 Tries Against – 3

Try Scorers: Cathy Boulton 8, Perise Ili 5, Tanya Osbourne 4, Bronwyn Laidlaw 4, Natalie Wanrooy 3, Denise Ututaonga-Scott 3, Florrie King 2, Vanessa Nootedoom 2, Julie Anne Columbus 2, Bronwyn Calvert 1, Bronwyn Hart 1, Deena Aitken 1, Maryanne Kearney 1, Jane Hamilton 1, Karen Bucholz 1, Jenny Beard 1, Selena Worsley 1, Pearl Palaialii 1.

Conversions: Perise Ili 12, Tanya Osbourne 8
Penalty Goals: Tanya Osbourne 4

*   *   *

At the completion of the presentation function and for the first time on tour the team cut loose with a few 'sickies' the next day.

Twelve Queensland players were selected in the Australian squad to play in the Test Match against New Zealand in Sydney on the 31st of August. Squad members from Queensland for the game were forwards; Julie Anne Columbus, Lisa Dwan, Mieke Gladwin, Shirley Russell, Lee Anne Wilkes and Selena Worsley and backs; Cathy Boulton, Bronwyn Calvert, Perise Ili, Bronwyn Laidlaw, Vanessa Nootedoom and Tanya Osbourne.

*   *   *

Records:

As it was the first National Interstate series almost all we achieved became history. It begs the question then, that after twenty-five years have some of the following statistics been surpassed?

Does 119 points scored in a single interstate match still stand as a record?

Is 119 points to 0 (from the same game) remain as the highest winning margin?

Is scoring 19 tries in a single match still a record?

Cathy Boulton (Queensland centre) scored six tries in this match; is it still the most tries scored by an individual in a single match?

*   *   *

15: The National Squad

When the National squad was trimmed to twenty-one Queensland lost another two players. On the run-on side in the Test match against New Zealand in August 1996, three Queensland players were reserves leaving seven members representing Australia.

It came back to me from several prominent people within the Australian managerial staff that the Queensland team in 1996, in their opinions were far superior to the Australian XV.

The New Zealand Silver Ferns defeated Australia 28-5.

* * *

Test matches New Zealand versus Australia:

1994 – New Zealand 39 defeated   Australia 0
1995 – New Zealand 37 defeated   Australia 0
1995 – New Zealand 67 defeated   Australia 0
1996 – New Zealand 28 defeated   Australia 5
1997 – New Zealand 40 defeated   Australia 0

* * *

Was Deena Aitken Queensland's first Wallaroo?

It must be noted that prior to the 1996 National Championships, Australian teams were selected on hearsay from Sydney, the ACT and Northern Territory selectors.

Some Queensland club members did play in the 1995 tests versus New Zealand (scores listed above). Queensland players randomly selected to play for Australia in these matches included Deena Aitken, Julie Anne Columbus, Lisa Dwan, Jane Hamilton and Charlie Beitzel.

16: Deplorable Coverage
– An Opportunity Lost

In the August issue of *'Rugby Review'*, Sara Dailey from New South Wales reviewed the Women's Rugby National Championships. I feel that the review should be repeated in this book.

'National Championships Review' — **Sarah Dailey**

"The National Women's Championships were held at Warringah Rugby Park in Sydney New South Wales from July 15th to the 21st. Queensland faced Northern Territory determined to reverse the result from Canberra last year (In 1995 the Northern Territory defeated the club side from Brisbane, Souths, representing Queensland in the final to win the National Championship 5-0). Northern Territory had the hardest task in defending their title against tough and ready teams from all other States and Territories. ACT led by captain Louise Ferris enter the National's this year ranked third behind Northern Territory and Queensland and were one of the most committed teams to take the field.

New South Wales under coach Rob Sawtell, performed exceptionally well at this year's Championships. Having already undertaken the selection pathway through a regular season, 'City versus Country' and a tour match against Alberta, this New South Wales team is easily the best we have seen.

Stronger competition was obvious this year due to a true Nationals format. State selections provide what a week of top-class competition between the teams with the first prize being the Champion State or Territory in Australia.

This prize could be sweetened even further for some players, whose successful performance at the Nationals will be a selection in the Australian Wallaroos, whose first challenge will be the third test against New Zealand in August."

I found this pathetic piece of coverage had to be answered and my letter to 'Rugby Review' was initiated thus;

"I found your article on women's rugby in the August issue compiled by Sarah Dailey as the most narrow-minded piece of reporting I have ever seen in your great magazine. Her article on the National Championships was a total disgrace considering this event was the greatest leap forward to date for women's rugby in Australia. If Sarah Dailey wishes to report on such events, she should ensure her articles are factual and unbiased."

My letter went on to give a total account of the National Championships. Other interesting statistics are portrayed in a previous chapter, 'The First Interstate Series'.

*   *   *

17: Return to Ballymore

Soon after the Queensland team returned home the QRU put on an evening of drinks and a presentation was held with State captain, Bronwyn Calvert presenting the National Champions Trophy to the QRU. Geoff Shaw related that the $50,000 the QRU invested into their State women's team had been totally justified.

"The Queensland Women's Rugby team was by far the most successful State representative team in 1996."

The QRU can be totally proud of their women's team.

The intentions of the QRU was to put more resources into women's rugby in 1997, thus raising the profile of women's rugby in Queensland. At the time I believed that the Queensland Rugby Union is doing more for women's rugby than any other body in Australia, although there were rumours that south of the border in New South Wales, their State union was setting up a high-profile intensity unit pertaining to women's rugby.

* * *

PART II
Lighter Times on Tour

'Ugly Day Competition':

These following events were the teams' initiation to break up the more serious aspects of competitive matches or morning team runs for the next match. The 'Ugly Day' was held on an afternoon and also ended in having the 'Des Kissane Cup' played dressed in the 'Ugly Day' outfit.

The 'Ugly Day' was pre-empted where all players and sporting team members had to pack in their kit the ugliest outfit to wear out on the day. An 'Ugly Outfit' competition was also awarded for the day's dress.

'Dickhead of the Day':

A 'Dickhead of the Day' was nominated daily, a court was held and the accused had to front the team. A nominated jury listened to the case in front of a chosen Judge and when found guilty had to pay a fine as nominated by the jury to our treasurer. All fines collected went into a pool to be spent at the conclusion of the National Championship. The following photos were taken in both the 1996 and 1997 events. The 'Dickhead of the Day ' had to wear a ridiculous hat for twenty-four hours, however had the honour of nominating the next day's victim.

Left: First 'Dick Head (DH) of the Day' 1996 tour. Queensland and Australian Half Back Karen Bucholz.

Centre: Even the Coach never escaped 'DH of the Day.' I was fined $20 for a crime I cannot remember, though more importantly, exempted from carrying the ridiculous handbag.

Right: Even our highest scoring winger never escaped the 'DH of the Day' award. In 1997, Cathy was fined for making an opposition fullback look ridiculous in defence.

At the first 'Ugly Day' competition held in 1996, the squad was broken up into four teams to contest the 'Des Kissane Cup' (Des was a full time QRU coach and was lent to us by QRU Director of Coaching, Duncan Hall on request for some coaching input. Des was invaluable to our team's build up in 1996 (thus the 'Ugly Day' competition was named after him). The games were played in the ugly day costumes as a novelty event.

*   *   *

The 1996 Teams Were:

Team 'Jonesy's Juveniles': — Louise Jones was our youngest member on tour (age 16) and was given the captaincy.

L-R: Denise Ututaonga-Scott, Mieke Gladwin, Louise Jones (c), Bronwyn Calvert, Moana O'Rourke and Perise Ili (missing).

*   *   *

Team 'Wilkes Wenches': — Lee Anne Wilkes (Queensland prop)

L-R: Jenny Beard, Selena Worsley, Natalie Wanrooy, Lee Anne Wilkes,
Lisa Dwan, Tanya Osbourne.

* * *

Team 'Pearl's Pansies': – Pearl Palaialii (Queensland/Australian Prop)

L-R: Vanessa Nootedoom, Shirley Russell, Jane Hamilton, Pearl
Palaialii (c), Maryanne Kearney, Cathy Boulton.

Note: Vanessa Nootedoom (left) wearing the 'DH of the day' hat. Vanessa was charged with 'crimes against humanity' in trampling her opposition five-eighth (New South Wales) without care or concern for the opposition's welfare. The sitting Judge for the day stated, *"It was an act of brutality."* The jury found her guilty and fined Vanessa one dollar.

* * *

Team 'Bus's Bitches': – Julie Anne Columbus aka Bus (Queensland/ Australian prop)

L-R: Bronwyn Laidlaw, Deena Aitken, Julie Anne Columbus, Karen Buchholz, Florrie King, Bronwyn Hart (missing).

* * *

Brisbane Club Members on Tour 1997 'Ugly Day':
"I'm sure the various rugby clubs in Brisbane would probably display team members photos as clubhouse mementos."

University of Queensland Team Members

L-R: Geoffrey Crowley (Physio), Karen Bucholz, Lee Anne Wilkes, Mieke Gladwin, Bronwyn Laidlaw, Cathy Boulton, Emily Stokes, Maryanne Kearney, Meredith Bochmann, Perise Ili.

*   *   *

Kenmore Bears (Ex-Souths) Members

L-R: Lisa Dwan, Tanya (Ossie) Osbourne, Pearl Palaialii, Debbie Grylls, Amanda Dinsdale, Moana O'Rourke, Selena Worsley, Bronwyn Hart.

Brothers and North Barbarians Members
L-R: Angie Patterson, Julie Anne Columbus (Bus), Jodie Kairl, Florrie
King, Cathy Olive, Jodie Collier (missing).

*　　*　　*

Voted as the best 'Uglies' on the day for 1997:

Left: Amanda Dinsdale (the ugly 'Ugly') and
Meredith Bochmann (the elegant 'Ugly').

Above: Queensland's Womens Rugby Squad 'Ugly Day'
Group Photo 1997 Adelaide

* * *

To my belief we were the only State/Territory team to participate in these types of fun days to break up the monotony of training/playing. On this occasion we had to pass the New South Wales team's billets to get to the ground on foot for our 'Ugly Day' and 'Des Kinnane Cup Day'.

The New South Wales team all came out of their billets to witness this strange passing of the Queensland team in total bewilderment. Nothing was said, I would suggest they just didn't believe what they were seeing.

* * *

At the 1997 Nationals we just split the squad up into the two teams with the captains being Maryanne Kearney (Queensland fullback) leading 'Kearney's Killers' and new (to be an Australian representative) halfback Debbie Grylls captaining 'Debbie's Druggies'.

Team 'Kearney's Killers' – 'Des Kinnane Cup' 'Ugly Day Adelaide 1997

Team 'Debbie's Druggies' – 'Des Kinnane Cup' 'Ugly Day Adelaide 1997

I named the positions players were appointed to with all forwards becoming backs (i.e., Props were now halfbacks, locks were now five-eighths etc) and all backs became forwards. The teams then had a warm up program with the backs having ten minutes prior to game commencement to sort out their scrums and lineouts. The game was played in 2 x 20 minutes halves culminating in an honourable drawn match.

Players warm up under the guidance of Karen Bucholz prior to the 'Des Kinnane Cup' in Adelaide 1997.

PART III
Queensland Women 1997

FRONT ROW (L-R): Carla Hardy (Manager), Tasi Woodard (Coach), Perise Ili, Florrie King Julie Ann Columbus (Captain), Cathy Boulton (V-. Captain), Debbie Grylls, Dean Patterson (Asst. Coach), Geoffrey Crowley (Physio)

SECOND ROW (L-R): Pearl Palaialii, Vanessa Nootedoom, Cathy Olive, Lisa Dwan, Mieke Gladwin, Bronwyn Laidlaw, Emily Stokes, Amanda Dinsdale, Moana O'Rourke, Selena Worsley

THIRD ROW (L-R): Karen Bucholz, lee Anne Wilkes, Bronwyn Hart, Tanya Osbourne, Meredith Bochmann, Jodie Collier, Angie Patterson

INSERTS: Jodie Kairl, Maryanne Kearney.

* * *

1: Losses and Gains

During the off-season and recommencement of the 1997 season we lost the following players from the 1996 Queensland representative team through overseas commitments, retirement, interstate relocation and injury.

Losses included Captain Bronwyn Calvert, Natalie Wanrooy, Denise Ututaonga-Scott, Jenny Beard, Jane Hamilton, Deena Aitken, Louise Jones and Shirley Russell. With gains in personnel including Debbie Grylls, Cathy Olive, Emily Stokes, Amanda Dinsdale, Meredith Bochmann, Jodie Collier, Angie Patterson and Jodie Kairl.

Sadly, we lost our inaugural captain Bronwyn Calvert while captaining the Australian Women's Rugby Union team which contested the first ever 'Women's Hong Kong Sevens' tournament in March 1997.

It was initially feared Bronwyn may never play rugby again. Following surgery and great determination her ambition was to be back training with the Australian (15 a side) squad by December in preparation for the 1998 Women's Rugby World Cup in Amsterdam, Holland.

Bronwyn moved to Sydney in April 1997 working as a dietitian for a nutrition company. She lives in Manly where she joined the Warringah Club and will train with the New South Wales squad when it reconvenes in December 1997.

New Queensland Members 1997

L-R: Meredith Bochmann, Angie Patterson, Emily Stokes, Debbie Grylls, Amanda Dinsdale, Jodie Collier, Cathie Olive (Missing: Jodie Kairl).

Debbie Grylls and Jodie Collier went on to represent Australia.

* * *

2: Refocusing and Integrating New Members

On reassembling the Queensland women's squad for 1997 we were fortunate enough to retain the following forwards from 1996, being; Julie Anne Columbus, Pearl Palaialii, Bronwyn Hart, Lisa Dwan, Mieke Gladwin (all now an International 'tight five') with Moana O'Rourke, Lee Anne Wilkes and Selena Worsley (Australian and International breakaway).

Amongst the backs we had Perise Ili, Cathy Boulton, Bronwyn Laidlaw, Tanya Osbourne, Karen Bucholz (now all International representatives) along with Florrie King, Vanessa Nootedoom and Maryanne Kearney.

By retaining sixteen members from the 1996 side, it was not hard to integrate the new players into our training and playing regime, introducing them into our 'four units' responsibilities with some players having multiple unit introduction.

The new forwards had to go through the rigorous scrum machine format with adjustments as required. Power scrummaging was one of the Queensland's team biggest assets and deterioration in this unit skill could not occur.

The merging of the new players into their respective units was made easier by my designating unit leaders, however an individual leader was not required in unit 1 as we now possessed an International 'tight five'. Selena Worsley was designated team leader in unit 2 as by now Selena, not only an International open side breakaway (wing forward) but the most lethal defensive forward in Australian women's rugby.

By moving former five-eighth Vanessa Nootedoom to No8 and with the introduction of two more wing forwards in Jodie Kairl and Jodie Collier, I with Selena had some work to do.

Following the 1997 National Championships our backrow forwards of Jodie Collier, Selena Worsley and Vanessa Nootedoom became the most dominating in the series.

Karen Bucholz now the Australian halfback took possession of the new halfback in Debbie Grylls (Kenmore Bears) and along with Cathy Boulton and Bronwyn Laidlaw, both University of Queensland players and now Internationals took ownership of 'Units 3 and 4' with another University player in fullback Maryanne Kearney looking after the new fullback Cathy Olive.

Left L-R: Jodie Collier, Vanessa Nootedoom and Selena Worsley.

Position wise, these three Back Row Forwards were a lethal 'Unit Two' in dominating Interstate Rugby. Australia's most devastating defensive forward was Selena Worsley.

At the final training sessions before games the 'four units' were isolated and under leaders would spend a final hour discussing their individual and 'unit' responsibilities for the coming game following team selection.

Our most versatile newcomer in Amanda Dinsdale, an outstanding athlete possessing all round skills, found herself playing in three 'units' being 'Units 2, 3 and 4' and would be more than capable of sitting in as lock. Amanda (aka 'Dingers') was above average height, fast and with exceptional ball skills and an all-round asset to any team.

Team training continued on a regular basis at Queensland's International rugby ground Ballymore for the 1997 National Championships to be hosted and played in Adelaide, South Australia.

* * *

3: A Supporting Loss

Former University, Queensland and Australian No8/Lock Duncan Hall, holding the position of Queensland Director of Coaching, initially invited me to raise and coach a Queensland women's team to participate in the inaugural Australian Interstate Championship to be held in Sydney in 1996. He gave me tremendous support in this program and was on call to assist me in any capacity I requested. He also, on a handshake gave me a three-year contract if I wished to commit myself to this period.

Unfortunately, Duncan left the QRU mid-season to take up an assistant coaching position with. ex-Australian coach Bob Dwyer, coaching a provincial side in the UK on Dwyer's invitation. The position of Queensland Director of Coaching was left vacant for the remainder of 1997.

Duncan's move would eventually lead to the termination of my coaching position with the Queensland women's team.

*   *   *

4: Captains in 1997

With the loss of Bronwyn Calvert (State Captain 1996) through injury and long-term rehabilitation, new appointments had to be made at the resumption of state training in 1997.

I offered the captaincy to Australian prop Julie Anne Columbus a veteran, also a very popular and admired player on both the Brisbane and Queensland scene. She had captained her club Barbarians since the inception of women's rugby in Brisbane and possessed leadership qualities players looked up to.

I invited Cathy Boulton to be vice-captain which she accepted.

I was fortunate enough to have many players with leadership qualities any of whom could and I am sure would have accepted the captaincy of this team including both locks Lisa Dwan and Mieke Gladwin, Bronwyn Laidlaw, Selena Worsley, Karen Bucholz and prop Lee Anne Wilkes a very under estimated leader and University of Queensland captain.

During the 1997 series held in Adelaide I was compelled to appoint three captains in Julie Anne Columbus, who stood down temporarily through injury thereby elevating vice-captain Cathy Boulton to the captaincy who when stood down for a match, backrow forward Selena Worsley led the Queensland team in a pool match versus the Northern Territory.

Left: Queensland had three Captains during the 'Australian National Championship' hosted by Adelaide, South Australia in 1997.

L-R: Selena Worsley (Wing/Forward), Julie-Anne Columbus (Prop) and Cathy Boulton (Centre) – All Internationals.

*　　*　　*

5: National Championships – Adelaide 1997

ollowing the inaugural championship in Sydney 1996, the stronger States and Territories were determined thus the two pools for the 1997 championship (6 – 13 July 1997) were split into the strong pool and the weaker pool from 1996.

The pools for 1997 were:

Pool 1:	Pool 2:
ACT	Western Australia
Northern Territory	Victoria
Queensland	South Australia
New South Wales	Australian Services Rugby Union

The two teams with the best 'for and against' would play off the National Championship.

Before departing Queensland, we were made aware of our Pool 1 draw. We would be playing in turn game one versus the ACT, game two versus the Northern Territory and game three playing New South Wales.

Before departing Queensland, we selected our first two teams and trained as selected at Ballymore. As it was a National selection series, I ensured all players would be exposed to the National selectors in our first two games. Following the 1996 series I believe the ACT was the second-best team in Australia so the team selected to play them was our most senior with our latest selections making up the bulk of the team against the Northern Territory, however interlaced with experience and a very strong reserve bench.

Game 1 versus the ACT:

Sensing the ACT team was not the drilled side of 1996 my opinion was justified when the Queensland forwards virtually took hold of the match from kick off. Our first try was scored by veteran half Karen Bucholz. Two of our new players in Amanda Dinsdale scored two tries and backrow forward Jodie Collier scored one. Tanya Osbourne, our outside centre scored two tries after lead up work by new inside centre vice-captain Cathy Boulton. Two tries were converted by Tanya Osbourne. The ACT failed to score securing our first win 34-0.

Scorers:

Tries: Amanda Dinsdale 2, Tanya Osbourne 2, Karen Bucholz 1 and Jodie Collier 1

Conversions: Tanya Osbourne 2

Game 2 versus the Northern Territory:

All our seven additions to 1997 participated in this match with Amanda Dinsdale (backing up from game one) scoring a try (now three tries in her first two games with Queensland). Debbie Grylls scored our first try with veteran and Australia's most dynamic breakaway, Selena Worsley scoring a try. A penalty goal and two conversions gave Queensland a comfortable 22-0 win.

Scorers:

Tries: Debbie Grylls, Amanda Dinsdale and Selena Worsley

Conversion: Debbie Grylls 2   Penalty Goal: Debbie Grylls 1

Game 3 versus New South Wales:

New South Wales had beaten both the ACT and Northern Territory in the pool matches so the final pool match was between two undefeated teams.

Perise Ili Queensland's five-eighth opened the scoring with a try following a huge forward surge upfield and with New South Wales going backwards, their defence could not apprehend a smart touchdown. Jodie Collier, breakaway scored a second try with centre Cathy Boulton's clever involvement scoring wide out. Finally, in their second year and third game scored their first try against Queensland. Bronwyn Laidlaw on the wing loped away outpacing pursuing defence to score her try out wide. Queensland 20 defeated New South Wales 7.

Scorers:

Tries: Perise Ili, Jodie Collier, Cathy Boulton and Bronwyn Laidlaw.

New South Wales converted try.

The two teams with the best 'for and against' were Queensland and New South Wales. The final to win the National Championship was to be played between these two teams.

* * *

National Championship Final:

In a spiteful match Queensland was awarded a penalty try to open the scoring with Tanya Osbourne kicking a penalty goal to hold an 8-0 half time score.

In the second half New South Wales scored an unconverted try closing the score to 8-5. We had worked for several days on a move from the lineout with the forwards taking the ball to centre field with our backline continuing to move across the field dragging the opposing backline with it. Our backrow forwards with our fullback have wonderful ball skills equivalent to our backs and formed up a second backline back on the blind side from where the lineout was initiated. Prop Lee Anne Wilkes took the ball from the forwards maul and broke back to and married up with our secondary backline with breakaway Selena Worsley running across an undefended try line. Lee Anne Wilkes was the prominent player in this movement and I'm sure Lee Anne will always remember the try set up by her that devastated the New South Wales team. We had practiced this move over two days but never used it prior to this match. That try was talked about well into the night of celebration following our winning the National Championship in both of its year's existence. Tanya Osbourne kicked another penalty goal to finalise the scores Queensland 16-5 .

Scorers:

Tries: Penalty try 1, Selena Worsley 1
Penalty goals: Tanya Osbourne 2
New South Wales try.

Championship Points in the Four Games played at the Nationals:

Points For: 92 Points Against: 12

Tries For: 15 Tries Against: 2

National Championship Scorers Queensland:

Tries: Amanda Dinsdale 3, Tanya Osbourne 2, Jodie Collier 2, Selena Worsley 2, Karen Bucholz 1, Debbie Grylls 1, Perise Ili 1, Cathy Boulton 1, Bronwyn Laidlaw 1, Penalty Try 1

Conversions: Tanya Osbourne 2, Debbie Grylls 2

Penalty Goals: Tanya Osbourne 2, Debbie Grylls 1

It may be noted that Western Australia was the only Australian team to score two tries against Queensland in any one game (game one during the 1996 series). Total games played during the 1996 and 1997 National Championships were eight.

*   *   *

Overdone:

Following all teams playing four games in a week the selectors not satisfied with what they had already seen decided to have a 'possibiles versus probables' match.

I objected to this as we were flying home Sunday morning and the 'University' team and 'Souths Maggies' had to play catch up club games on the Sunday afternoon. The plea fell on deaf ears.

So, as an alternative I suggested that a match, Queensland versus a 'Rest of Australia' team be played. After a quick discussion by the selectors this suggestion was negated as I'm sure they knew what the outcome would be. The proposed game was cancelled.

6: A Queensland Selector

The late Stan Pilecki was requested to attend the Adelaide 1997 Australian Women's Rugby Interstate Championship as a selector representing Queensland.

On our return to Queensland, I was seated next to Stan on the aircraft and asked him how the National selections turned out. Stan looked at me and shook his head, the conversation went thus;

"Tasi, it was the greatest waste of time and farce I've ever been involved in. Following the selection of the National squad there were twelve Queenslanders in that squad."

The National selectors were Shelly Lingman (coach of the Northern Territory), a female representing New South Wales, the National coach from the ACT and Stan.

When the selection process was completed one selector stated, *"We have no representation from West Australia."*

"Who is their best player?" was the question put.

A player was named and Stan asked, *"Well how will you fit her in?"*

The reply was, *"Well Queensland has twelve representatives, drop a Queensland player."*

Then the selection committee discovered no Victorian player was selected. The women stated that they wanted an Australian squad where all states were represented .

Stan then asked, *"Well how are you going to fit her in?"* dreading the forthcoming reply.

"Drop another Queenslander as they still have eleven players in the squad."

Stan said he exploded stating, "Now wait. When you select a squad to represent Australia all State identity ceases. It is now an Australian team and initially we have selected the best players available regardless of State representation ... this process is ludicrous."

The selection committee insisted an all-State representation.

I then asked Stan, "Who were the two Queensland players dropped to make way for a West Australian and Victorian player?"

Stan replied, "I do not know. I stood up from the table and stated I want no further participation in this farce. Do not ever request me to partake in this process again," and left.

To this day I have no knowledge of the two Queensland players who were deleted from the initial National squad. We may have had two more Internationals.

*   *   *

7: The National Trophy

The Queensland Women's Rugby team again being undefeated in the 1997 National Championship series was once again presented with the National Trophy at the Saturday evening function following the week-long Championship series.

The Queensland team had the trophy in its possession Sasturday night, however when preparing for the travel home on the Sunday morning the trophy could not be located. Sadly, we returned to Brisbane without it and obviously could not pass it onto the QRU at Ballymore. Several months later a large package was delivered to the QRU containing the National Trophy sent from Darwin.

If the QRU ever received an explanation from the Northern Territory of them being in possession of it, it was never passed on to myself or the team.

I may note that at the presentation the South Australian Rugby Union presented a 'Series Winning' medal to the Queensland squad. It was a very impressive inscribed medallion hung by a ribbon of the South Australian colours of navy-blue, gold and red. I still have the medallion in my possession ... thank you South Australian rugby.

* * *

8: From Maroon to
Gold and Green

In the two years of 1996 and 1997, fifteen Queensland women players represented Australia at International level in rugby union, being;

Cathy Boulton, Karen Bucholz, Bronwyn Calvert, Julie Anne Columbus, Lisa Dwan, Mieke Gladwin, Debbie Grylls, Bronwyn Hart, Perise Ili, Bronwyn Laidlaw, Vanessa Nootedoom, Tanya Osbourne, Pearl Palaialii, Shirley Russell and Selena Worsley.

The front row props of Julie Anne Columbus and Pearl Palaialii with hooker Bronwyn Hart, along with locks Lisa Dwan and Mieke Gladwin completed a 'tight five'. Backrow forwards of Selena Worsley, Shirley Russell and #8 Vanessa Nootedoom rounded off a full International pack.

Two halfbacks in veteran Karen Bucholz and Debbie Grylls with Perise Ili completed the halves. Four centres in Bronwyn Calvert, Tanya Osbourne, Cathy Boulton (also representing on the wing) and Bronwyn Laidlaw (centre, wing and fullback such was her versatility).

A player whom I felt should have represented Australia was 'University of Queensland' and Queensland fullback Maryanne Kearney.

Mary Anne in my opinion was the best defensive fullback in Australia as she was never caught out of position and was very secure under the high ball. She initiated many counter attacks from primary fullback and also successfully timed her entry on many occasions, into backlines leading to scoring opportunities. I would not have exchanged Maryanne Kearney for any fullback in Australia.

*   *   *

9: Their Greatest Challenge
29th July 1997:

Following the National Championship in Adelaide earlier in 1997, the United States of America's National Women's Rugby team were locked into a four-game tour of Australia in the later part of July. Their tour itinerary consisted of:

Game 1: versus the ACT, Canberra

Game 2: versus New South Wales, Sydney

Game 3: versus Queensland 'Ballymore' Brisbane

Game 4: versus Australia 'Suncorp Stadium' Brisbane

Game 4 versus Australia was to be a curtain raiser to the Tri-Nations match Australia versus South Africa at 'Suncorp Stadium'.

The United States team had attended the first two Women's Rugby World Cups and had established themselves as No2 in the world behind the No1 ranked New Zealand 'Silver Ferns' (who had won both World Cups).

Training at Ballymore continued for the Queensland women's team with the realisation that we were to play against a fully International team who were ranked #2 in the world.

This was to be a test of 'How good are we?' as to date including our first game ever, against a Canadian team, I felt we had never really been challenged.

I rang the National Women's coach in Canberra and requested from him a tape of the USA's first game versus the ACT, which in due course was forwarded to me. The United States defeated the ACT 45-0.

On receiving the tape USA versus ACT, I studied the game and then replayed it. I came to the conclusion that if the USA did not have a 'Plan B' they could be in trouble when playing Queensland.

My next move was to sit down at Ballymore with the Queensland team and replay the match again initially pointing out to the team that their game plan played straight into one of our greatest strengths, our backrow forwards. We were going to have a 'ball' led by Australia's most devastating open side breakaway in Selena Worsley and her co-backrow partners in the solid and strong No8 Vanessa Nootedoom and Jodie Collier, an outstanding backrow.

It did not take long into the replay where I had to no longer point out their (the USA's) deficiencies versus our strengths as this team through two seasons had the ability to size up opposition's frailties, they were a seasoned team. I felt a sense of high spirits and positive anticipation to the forthcoming match, which was vividly clear when team training resumed on the main oval at Ballymore, at last we were going to know exactly where we stood in the women's rankings of rugby.

The United States match versus New South Wales was a surprise as I expected New South Wales would extend the USA though not to be. The USA defeated New South Wales 31-6 with New South Wales scoring two penalty goals. I never got to view that match not that it would have altered much, our game plan would not change.

I rang the Australian Women's coach and National selector to fly up for the match. I would pick him up at the airport, accommodate him and return him to the airport for his flight to Canberra. He declined the offer. How strange the National Women's Rugby coach and selector not wishing to attend the USA versus Queensland match prior to the Australia versus USA International?

The Ballymore match was a 'double header.' The opening match was to be played between the Queensland B team 'The Blue Heelers' and a Japanese B team followed by the Queensland versus USA women's match, so a good attendance was expected.

From the Queensland squad of twenty-four players, I was informed that I could use only twenty-one. Two players were not available and poor Jodie Kairl was told to turn up in her Queensland tracksuit but would not be allowed to play. I also informed the team that I intended to play all twenty-one players as they could all claim to have participated in this historic match.

As anticipated a large crowd had arrived at Ballymore to witness both games, easily the largest crowd our team was to perform in front of. It was the Queensland women's team's tenth game in two years however only the second in Queensland with the Canadian's Alberta team being their first ever match in 1996.

I observed the USA team's arrival and I was surprised at their lack of size in comparison to the larger Queensland team, especially the Queensland forwards. I mentally noted that the USA team was going to have a hard night in the scrums and we were going to establish a physical domination from the very first scrum. The USA team was allocated Ballymore #2 oval for their pre-game warm up and the Queensland team had Ballymore #3.

From our inaugural team in 1996 I laid down a pre-game drills session which was carried out and finishing with a series of running passing skills under congested conditions. For the later part of our pre match drills I had noticed that USA Women's coach accompanied by two American males had made their way over to us and was observing our very clinical drills. I was in their close proximity and as yet they did not know who I was and I heard the coach state to her male companions, *"I have bad vibes about this game,"* then moved on back to their team.

I did not pass this little statement on to the team as I did not want overconfidence to enter into their minds.

Back into the dressing rooms and after the USA team had run onto Ballymore our huddled circle recited as before all games:

> *"We are Queensland*
> *We are history*
> *We are family*
> *We are as one*
> *We are Queensland*
> *I am Queensland"*

These were always the last words spoken before running onto the field of play, however I had a little more to add, *"You have the opportunity to become the first Australian team to defeat a full International team that are No2 in the world rankings."*

"Tasi get the Queensland team onto the field," a voice rang out from outside the dressing room door.

The Queensland team ran onto Ballymore in front of a large crowd, who gave them a tremendous ovation. They were about to witness their state side which they had heard so much about, however had never seen them play.

The USA kicked off, a Queensland forward caught the ball ran forward to contact the opposition, set up a maul with fellow forwards and with the second pass from the maul was deemed a forward pass, a USA scrum, almost programmed. On the ball being put into the scrum the Queensland forwards gave an eight-person coordinated 'snap shove'. The USA scrum, like I have never seen before, just went up in the air and backwards. Their front row was penalised for disengaging and standing upright, attempting to stabilise their scrum, too late as they had no hope of stopping their backward progress. The physical domination was asserted, not surprisingly as I believe our pack was an average eight to nine kilos per person heavier and with their fine-tuned coordinated skills, one side was overwhelmed with success and the other devastated and humiliated.

The first thought that came to my head was, *"I wonder if one of our forwards had an orgasm?"* We had become so proficient at demolishing opposition scrums.

With forward domination it was not long before our halfback in Karen Bucholz scored our first try. A second was scored by winger Amanda Dinsdale within a few minutes of resumption of play.

With the USA getting some ball possession and having their inside backs tackled before reaching their gain line by our ever-eager backrow forwards, who were relishing in the prior knowledge of their game plan. Much on field discussion was held by the USA team during stoppages of play, however it came to note that they did not have a 'Plan B' in their game repertoire. Soon after a third try was scored by centre Tanya Osbourne following a successful lineout, who converted her own try.

Above: Mieke Gladwin was Queensland's and eventually Australia's primary line out exponent. Here Mieke has no trouble winning a lineout against New South Wales.

Mieke was also a mobile forward with outstanding skills. Her along with Second Row partner Lisa Dwan became Australia's Second Row pairing.

All through this article I have talked on the emphasis we put on our scrummaging, however we also worked on our lineout skills constantly. Having both locks in Mieke Gladwin (who became Australia's primary lineout exponent) along with her lock partner Lisa Dwan another very capable lineout jumper (both Australian locks) we were never threatened by any team in two years. Lineout domination was also a key to our success through this unit skill superiority.

Amanda Dinsdale scored her second try of the match giving Queensland a healthy 22-0 half time lead.

I ran out our strongest fifteen for commencement of play less our primary fullback Maryanne Kearney, who was absent for her brother's overseas wedding.

With a commanding half time lead my rotation of players commenced early in the second half giving our six reserves game participation as promised.

The USA finally scored an unconverted try by kicking wide to their wing and winning the race to the in-goal ball.

Queensland replied with a try by backrow forward Jodie Collier and converted by Tanya Osbourne. I may add that this try was scored following the USA attempting to clear the ball by kicking from just outside their own goal line. Jodie took the ball on the full and after sidestepping several defenders touched down alongside the goal posts (29-5).

The USA scored their second try under similar circumstances to their first, kick and chase. I must admit they did possess pace in their outside backs (29-10).

It became apparent to the USA that territory gainage could only be achieved by kicking when in possession. This aspect of play by oppositions was not new to us. Thus, they became only the second team to score two tries in a game against Queensland in two years.

Meredith Bochmann scored the final try of the match. I wish to talk on Meredith's try as it was one of the most spectacular individual tries, I have ever witnessed in 40 years of rugby involvement.

Pressing the USA in their own twenty-five metre area with them in possession they kicked the ball downfield into the Queensland half. Meredith on the wing caught it on the full in flight and sprinted the ball back into the USA half, changed direction and ran into centre field. Still going forward, she kicked the ball in an up and under to her opposite wing, followed her kick and without changing pace leapt high caught the ball on the full and was not apprehended on her journey to the try line wideout.

A deservedly standing ovation from the grandstand by the crowd was justified. I mentally noted that Meredith had kicked the ball in a 'no kick zone,' however I forgave her immediately.

Final Score: Queensland 34 defeated USA 10
Scorers:
Tries: Amanda Dinsdale 2, Karen Bucholz, Tanya Osbourne, Jodie Collier, Meredith Bochmann
Conversions: Tanya Osbourne 2
USA: Tries 2

The Queensland team departed the Ballymore field with the USA team to a standing ovation. In the dressing room there were all hugs and kisses. The Queensland team had become the first Australian team to defeat an International team being the

USA, ranked No.2 in the world. However, the main subject of conversation was on Meredith Bochmann's outstanding try.

Afterwards in the reception room a high ranking QRU official approached me and said, *"Congratulations Tasi, that was the first game of women's rugby I have watched, I was only going to watch it for a while, however I became so engrossed in the game I couldn't leave it. I had no idea that women could play to that level of rugby and to watch running rugby was very special."*

Several other QRU officials also congratulated me on the game, they also conveyed how the game was a wonderful spectacle.

I think it was just dawning on the QRU, that Queensland rugby possessed something special and for the second year running their women's team was again the most successful Queensland representative team.

During the reception, the Australian Women's Rugby team was announced for the International test Australia versus USA as a 'curtain raiser' at 'Suncorp Stadium' to the Tri-Nations match Australia versus South Africa.

The USA coach (who now knew who I was) sidled up to me and asked, *"Tasi, how many Queensland players are in the Australian team?"*

My reply, *"Four in the run-on side."*

The USA coach responded, *"Thank God for that."*

The penny had finally dropped why the Australian coach nor any National selectors attended our game ... the Australian team had been selected prior to our match.

"How many tickets do you want for the game?" I was asked ... my reply, *"None!"*

*   *   *

In the Test match at 'Suncorp Stadium' the USA defeated Australia 28-24.

The USA tour Australia in 1997

USA defeated ACT 45-0

USA defeated New South Wales 31-6

USA lost to Queensland 10-34

USA defeated Australia 28-24

* * *

A little more maroon in the gold and green may have seen Australia win their first International match.

* * *

10: Round Up

I doubt in any other sport any team could have achieved what this outstanding team did so when a provincial level competition was initiated. Once again it was an experience and education, they gave me being involved with women in sport to whom I shall forever be indebted to. I shall never forget the individuals and successes they achieved in 1996 and 1997.

Queensland's points for and against 1997

Points for: 126 against 22   Tries for: 21 against 4

Queensland's points for and against 1996

Points for: 262 against 18   Tries for: 42 against 3

Queensland's points for and against 1996 and 1997

Points for: 388 against 40   Tries for: 63 against 7

Average per Game (10)

Points for: 38.8 Points against: 4.0   Tries for: 6.3 Tries against: 0.7

At the beginning of 1998 Gavin Head had been given the position of Director of Coaching of the QRU.

He requested a meeting at Ballymore with me believing he wanted to go over my coaching agenda with the Queensland

Women's team for the coming season. Not so ... Gavin indicated my position would be open to his decision.

I explained in 1996 the then Queensland Director of Coaching, Duncan Hall had verbally given me a three-year position in coaching on a handshake. Gavin Head said he had no evidence of this agreement and my position would be looked at.

When I was Director of Coaching and selector with Southern Districts Club, Annerley I had several discussions with Gavin in reference to his positional elevation within the club, which was not to his satisfaction. Here it was eighteen years later — 'pay back'.

My position as coach with the Queensland Women's Rugby team was terminated by a letter from Gavin Head on behalf of the Queensland Rugby Union. I appealed this decision directly to the CEO of Queensland Rugby Union; however, he did have the decency to phone me and explain that coaching appointments within the QRU was the sole responsibility and decision of the Director of Coaching QRU.

So ended a remarkable two years and I must admit enjoyable association with an outstanding team.

Au revoir rugby — Mieke Gladwin R.I.P.

* * *

11: A Pleasant Reward

At the turn of this century an Australian medal was struck to commemorate the new century (Millennium medal) an Australian sporting achievement 'The Australian Sports Medal.'

To

CLIFFORD WALTER WOODARD

Greeting

WHEREAS Her Majesty Queen Elizabeth The Second, Queen of Australia, has instituted an Australian medal to commemorate, in the year 2000, Australian sporting achievement; I DO by this warrant award you the Australian Sports Medal.

Governor-General of the
Commonwealth of Australia

By His Excellency's Command

Prime Minister

I was awarded the medal for forty-one years dedication to rugby 1957 to 1997 as a player, captain, captain/coach, coach, administration and finally coaching.

My initial problem was to find out where it fitted with military medals.

Personalities who received 'The Australian Sports Medal' in 2000 for rugby involvement included John Eales, Michael Lynagh and David Campese – *"I was in good company."*

*   *   *   *

PART IV
The Brisbane Scene

An Australian Women's National selector came up from Canberra to attend the 'Queensland Club Championship' to assess the strength of Queensland women's rugby and individual performances. At the completion of the State final played between 'University of Queensland' and 'Souths' he approached me and stated, *"There are no club sides in Australia that can play with the intensity of University and Souths."*

* * *

Foreword

*'*The Brisbane Scene' covers the Brisbane women's rugby competition, however is mainly dedicated to the two 'powerhouse' teams of the Brisbane competition. Firstly the 'University of Queensland' team who dominated the competition unbeaten in grand finals in the short history of the Women's Rugby competition and 'Southern Districts Maggies' named after the clubs 'Souths Magpies.'

Between these two outstanding teams they provided eighteen of the twenty-four members (University with ten and South's eight) for the inaugural Queensland State team to participate in the first Australian Interstate National Championship.

Their inter club rivalry was very intense to the point where every match was for competition and ladder supremacy.

In 1996 including the pre-season matches, the 'Crosby Cup,' 'Queensland Club Championship' and 'The National Mutual Cup'

(Brisbane competition) University and Souths met on seven occasions, with Souths winning four of these encounters and University three. These losses being the only losses suffered by these two teams for the duration of the 1996 season.

* * *

Ten members from the 'University of Queensland Rugby Union' club were selected for the inaugural State side.

Back Row (L-R): Bronwyn Laidlaw (Fullback, Centre, Wing), Deena Aitken (No8), Jenny Beard (Wing), Maryanne Kearney (Fullback), Mieke Gladwin (Lock)

Front Row (L-R): Cathy Boulton (Centre, Wing), Karen Bucholz (Halfback), Natalie Wanrooy (Breakaway), Perise Ili (Five eight), Lee Anne Wilkes (Prop).

Six of these players in (Forwards) Aitken, Gladwin and (Backs) Boulton, Bucholz, Ili and Laidlaw would go on to represent Australia.

*   *   *

Eight members from the 'Southern Districts Rugby Union' club were selected for the inaugural State side.

Back Row (L-R): Lisa Dwan (Lock), Bronwyn Hart (Hooker), Selena Worsley (Breakaway), Moana O'Rourke (Prop)

Front Row (L-R): Pearl Palaialii (Prop), Bronwyn Calvert (Centre), Tanya Osbourne (Centre), Shirley Russell (Breakaway).

Seven of these members in (Forwards) Dwan, Hart, Palaialii, Russell, Worsley and (Backs) Calvert and Osbourne would go on to represent Australia.

*   *   *

1: Background

In early January 1996 if anyone would have suggested to me that I would be involved in women's rugby within a month I would have suggested to them that they should; see a psychiatrist, get off Prozac or simply had been indulging too much of our favourite Queensland refreshment XXXX (Fourex).

By end of January the reality of such a scenario was quite tangible, however I was still hesitant of making a commitment beyond assisting in some part time capacity.

* * *

In mid-January I received a phone call from Christine (Goldie) Gold, who for the past several seasons of women's rugby in Brisbane was Souths' women's team manager and also the manager of the Australian women's team's first overseas tour to New Zealand in 1995.

Goldie explained that a Souths' committee member had suggested she should give me a ring to request by any chance I could give some assistance to the Souths' women's team in any coaching capacity for the 1996 season. She explained, as women's rugby was a fledgling sport not only in Brisbane and Australia, but we also were the last major rugby nation yet to recognise and address women's rugby. That observation was supported by the fact that during the Australian women's tour to New Zealand in 1995 for the one-off test, the New Zealand side easily defeated Australia 64-0.

In 1994 they had been defeated in Australia by New Zealand 39-0.

Goldie's major concern was that the women's teams in Brisbane could not secure coaches with the experience in that field to give a reasonable time allocation to assist or impart a high level of rugby knowledge amongst their ranks. This would raise the standard the game where it could be more generally accepted by the rugby fraternity. It was also apparent to Goldie that most clubs were not interested or supportive in attempting to secure coaches that could lift the standard of rugby at this level.

Now my concept of women's rugby was perhaps on a parity with 95% of the rest of the Australian male population, a 'touch and giggle' affair to be tolerated because it was there. And to this, firmly believing that the female participants were all born in families consisting of five or more children with them being the only female and was forced to play backyard rugby, under threat of violence, against their brothers, thus being subject to a very physical upbringing. Other reflections one could conjure up for reasons in women selecting to participate in this collision sport are; they had been brought up on 'Rambo' movies; women who simply hated all other women and rugby being a means where they could legally beat hell out of each other without fear of arrest or apprehension; they simply had a violent husband/boyfriend and it was a method in which they could learn the art of violent aggression with the prospective recipient not being aware of what was taking place.

I listened to Goldie's compassionate pleas and I did admire her persistence along with her projected dedication to the cause. She informed me of a women's team meeting to be held at Souths club the following Sunday, a pre-season team get together and an administration chat.

I reluctantly agreed to attend, simply just as a silent observer, however I would not make any commitment at that point in time. In retrospect I believe Goldie had cleared a hurdle when I promised to attend.

*   *   *

2: The Meeting

In late January I attended the Souths' women's rugby team meeting held at their clubhouse.

I attended as a casual observer, interested to hear what women talk about in conjunction with our great game and what motivates them and draws them to and wanting to participate in this collision sport. A quick headcount confirmed seventeen players were in attendance with three apologies so at least they could field a team. I later learnt that this was an extremely hard objective to achieve by most Brisbane suburban teams with the exception of the University of Queensland team (premiers in the first seasons), who had a large player base to tap, the envy of all other clubs.

The meeting was presided by Bronwyn Calvert, a very attractive lady, whom by profession is a nutritionist and through that position was very adept in speaking to audiences. She gave a very in-depth presentation on the approaching 1996 season, their realistic goals and other administrative matters.

In the first two seasons of Brisbane women's rugby, Souths came third on both occasions behind University and Norths Barbarians and it was Souths' desire to improve their position to the detriment of the teams above them. In observing the audience from the background, I realised that the group possessed many attractive women, quite athletic in appearance, seemed dedicated and possessed a desire to better themselves. I was not sure whether this portrayed determination was simply an early season hype or a genuine desire. It was still beyond my comprehension why these women wished to participate in such a physical contact sport such as rugby. My comprehension also accepted women as soft delicate persons and their sporting prowess should be kept to non-contact sport.

At the conclusion of the meeting, I was introduced to Bronwyn and some other senior members of the team. I was still unsure whether I should enter into this new world of rugby. The senior members explained that they simply had an individual and team desire to be better rugby players on all levels and required a coach who was capable to impart that knowledge and was also capable of putting it into practice on the field of play.

I have always been a sentimentalist and I thought if I possessed that knowledge and the capabilities to assist their earnest desire then I had nothing to lose by attempting to assist their team. I decided to compromise. I would attend training sessions and coach and after a month if both parties were compatible to each other I would reassess my position.

We departed Souths with me agreeing to attend the first training session, which just happened to be the next evening (Monday night). While I was walking home, as I lived quite close to Souths, I was contemplating the afternoon events and thought, *"Shit! What have I got myself into?"*

* * *

3: A Sensitive Area?

In a meeting with Bronwyn Calvert (Souths Maggies' captain) I requested from her the club's history with their team. She replied they had a very poor relationship with the Souths Club. The women's team was accepted, however ignored and not supported in any capacity.

In previously requesting for a coach, they would be allocated someone who had applied for a coaching position within Souths and after being denied a position in the top five grades or the three 'Colts' teams would be allocated to the women's team. The coach was unacceptable. Some of the coaches, who were given the position were there for alternative reasons and had to be dismissed. Team training was mostly carried out by her and senior players.

I had a first-hand experience of the attitude towards their women players well into the season proper when utilising the club for a playing member's 21st birthday party. A very senior committee member sidled up to me and asked, "*How many 'dykes' in your team Tasi?*" I looked him in the eye and asked, "*How many 'poofters' in Souths?*" He walked away.

Bronwyn also told me in a previous season when all the Colts teams have been eliminated from the finals had their 'Mad Monday' end of season party at the clubhouse as the women's team were training for their upcoming semi-final. They were confronted from the clubhouse veranda by many young drunks yelling obscenities and making vile suggestions to their team members to such an extent that the women just packed up and left the premises.

By the end of the season of 1996, Southern Districts Rugby Union Club had within their women's team, eight Queensland representative players and from them seven International players. Still the respect did not eventuate which would in turn explode within the district club's face. This event is mentioned in a later chapter.

* * *

4: First Training Session

'Relationship — February 1996'
"I am not treating you as women, I am treating you as rugby players."

In retrospect, one of the wisest utterances I made easing myself into the world of women's rugby, as they had been attempting to get themselves recognised as rugby players, not simply as women attempting to play rugby.

*   *   *

The next day I pondered on how I should approach this new direction in my life and after much contemplation I could only conclude, and perhaps wisely, to treat it exactly as I would if it was the first training session of the year with a male team.

"I am not treating you as women, I am treating you as rugby players" … seventeen nods of acknowledgement.

"I'm not here to get you fit, that is an individual commitment. I'm here initially to teach you correct basic skills and the simple fundamentals in producing better individual players thus making this a better skilled team" … seventeen nods of acknowledgement.

"I'm not here to run the guts out of you simply because running is rugby, if so, you will do it with a ball in hand, in committing yourself to a skill

or running in grids, working in condensed traffic to develop ball skills, running skills, evasion skills and teamwork" ... seventeen nods of acknowledgement.

"I must confess to you that I am basically a defensive coach. My attitude in rugby is, if an opposition cannot score against you, they will not defeat you. I would prefer to win a game 5-0 than 30-25" ... seventeen nods of acknowledgement.

"Ball skills, running skills, passing variations, coordination, understanding and communication are the 'bread and butter' issues of rugby. We must pursue these skills relentlessly. We're going to do the simple things well"... seventeen nods of acknowledgement.

"I have produced for you an endurance fitness program, the type of fitness we must concentrate on initially in the season. No one will oversee you on this program, it is an individual commitment. However, as the season progresses it will become evident who had been following the program"... seventeen nods of acknowledgement.

"For tonight's training, following warm up and a stretching program, we will concentrate on variations of passing skills coordinating key factors, followed by some grid work utilising passing skills and finally we will concentrate on basic ripping techniques pertaining to maul ball"... seventeen nods of acknowledgement.

At the completion of our first night's training, I produced some papers requesting players to write their name and preferred playing position followed by their secondary position. I then explained that players would be broken up into 'Units 1 – 4' according to their preferred position and they would commence training with players compatible to their unit so as to initiate a working relationship with players they're operating next to in the game situation.

Walking home I felt very comfortable with the team's reaction to night one. One area that really surprised me was the individual's skill level which two hours earlier I never would have believed existed. On night one there was a definite willingness to do the hard work, a competitive attitude existed, discipline evident and the individual's receptiveness to constructive criticism. Even then I had the suspicion that I was working with some exceptionally fine athletes.

I was thinking, *"If their enthusiasm and dedication continues"* ...

*   *   *

At a very early meeting with Bronwyn Calvert, I requested her to explain to me how they previously prepared for matches on game days. She responded that when a team arrived for a game, they would then decide who is playing in what position depending on the availability of players.

Ongoing through players responses in requesting their preferred position and following training and early season trials I began marrying up the individual's capabilities to organise a balanced team. With some there needed no discussion, they being made for their preferred position. Players removed from their preferred position I individually took aside and explained the reasoning for the shift and surprisingly the most common response was, *"Whatever is best for the team. I don't mind."*

With this kind of response, I began feeling our bonding was cementing into a very sound relationship.

5: Dick and I

I have spent many years involved with Golden Oldies/Veterans rugby having played in England, Canada, New Zealand, Sweden, Ireland and quite a few other international venues. During my time indulging in this great concept, you meet many people from all corners of the globe one such character and a very close friend is a fellow ex-prop in Dick Rutledge, a Kiwi who for many years represented Canterbury (New Zealand) at provincial level.

Being ex-props Dick and I have endured quite a few games together and against one another, but always share the most important aspect of our games together, the after-game functions that usually extend far into the night. Chattering about anything and everything that the exclusive club of fellow props talk about as no one else knows, only we know, who are the good and bad ones and also the pretenders.

Following a Golden Oldies Festival, the 'Waitangi Day Festival' in February 1996 at Redlands and after the games and hard into the serious side of the festival and very late at night as the time wore on, I suspected Dick had something serious on his mind which he wished to relate to me about, however could not bring himself to broach this sensitive issue. I never attempted to intrude into his inner thoughts, however I knew a few more XXXX would loosen lips I thought would be the appropriate manner.

Sometime later Dick sheepishly looked at me and said, *"Tasi* if I tell you something in confidence will you promise not to laugh at me or tell anyone else at this point in time?”

“Certainly Dick. Tell me. My lips are sealed” I replied.

“Well, Tasi I don’t know how to tell you this or what you may think of me” …

“Come on Dick let’s have it.”

“Well, Tasi I’m going to coach a women’s rugby team … Sunnybank.”

I immediately burst into laughter, more of relief than any other reason. All night long I was contemplating how I was going to tell my fellow prop I was also. Souths Maggies and the Sunnybank women’s teams now had a great relationship.

*   *   *

6: A New Coaching Challenge

Having eighteen years in a playing and captain/coaching capacity through the sixties, seventies and eighties and with that experience behind me I believed transferring this experience to a women's team would be one of simplicity, however I soon learnt that I must alter and rethink many attitudes in coaching application because of the physical strength differences in male and female players and some of the basic skill deficiencies in comparison due to the strength factor.

My first awareness was due to the lack of strength in the wrist, arms and shoulders thus passing skills were reduced greatly creating a more condensed game. Condensed games on any level become messy affairs. There was also a huge difference in ball retention/security thereby lacking continuity in play. The ability to successfully have continuity in play also generates huge team confidence and morale.

An input of unit skills coordination and support was a major priority. The other huge gap in male/female skill levels, which quickly became evident was kicking skills. Most women have difficulty in kicking the ball out on the full from the centre of the ground let alone making ground gain for the ensuing lineout.

From what one had taken for granted just did not exist. These and smaller challenges came to surface as training continued early in the season, however all team/individual deficiencies can be overcome.

I talked to Bronwyn Calvert on these deficiencies and she took it on her own back to set up strength tests and weight programs for the individuals. Becoming stronger was a vital ingredient in enhancing passing skills and within several months these benefits became evident. This skill combined with other skills, positional play and the support factor enabled us to create an expansive game to the extent that we could play a game from sideline to sideline. The condensed game was a thing of the past for the Maggies.

With regards to the second deficiency mentioned we devised other methods of taking advantage of penalties from the centre of the ground. The method employed did have advantages, firstly, of the ball not finding touch had been eliminated and secondly, we retained possession. Tap and run in a constructed team movement.

In my first coaching session with the Maggies, I declared that the team would concentrate on basics and until basics and a degree of competence was attained, we would not progress into the deeper complexities of the game. I envisaged that we would not progress from basic, unit or team skills training until the season proper commenced. All along attitudes in coaching had to be addressed and altered in conjunction with the 'difference factor'. Application to these alterations where in most cases very simple and with very little adjustments, were found to have their advantages also.

I believe a huge advantage I had at my disposal was that I possessed a team of athletes who had a desire to be the best in their chosen sport and had never been subjected to a series of coaches over the short years of their development.

With males their rugby training is initiated in 'under sixes or sevens' and as they get older and move up the grades and by the time, they reach maturity and senior grade level they have been subjected to many coaches, a variety of coaching methods and have been implemented a comparison factor, which becomes evident. By the time they arrive at senior level most players have a very in-depth knowledge of the game and will reject some coaches' methods of unit or team skills play or game plan as they may believe a method by an earlier coach would be more advantageous or superior, thus a rejection factor may mentally occur. The 'we could do this better' mentality is ever present.

In my case I had a team, never being coached beyond the simplistics of the game, having a huge hunger for knowledge, a desire in being the best and a willingness to put all aspects of my coaching into practice. They were willing subjects and devoid of the 'comparison factor' from previous coaches. Above all they believed in what I was portraying and as pre-season matches were having outstanding results their confidence grew and their achievements resulted in the team accepting that 'what we are doing is correct'.

The loyalty I had for these athletes was reciprocal.

Passed on in April 96 – 'Dedication'

"If Tasi told me to jump off the Story Bridge I would do it without question as, I know it would be the right thing to do." – Related by Tasi's wife Ailsa as commented by a player.

As the early season training progressed my emphasis was on defence practiced by having the four units playing in game situation against one another and in attack emphasising our game around the four team principles:

1: Go Forward

2: Support

3: Continuity, and

4: Pressure

They soon became aware that if they were not the ball carrier they were not out of the game as they had an obligation to position themselves to be a supportive player or putting themselves in readiness for the next phase of play.

They also realised a fitness level was required to get themselves to the gain line in defence before the opposition, in ball possession, could advance the ball to the gain line. We had to maintain our strengths while improving and working on our weaknesses.

The method of coaching this team was carried over to the Queensland representative team and noting the points for and against with the Maggies in 1996 and Queensland in 1996 and 1997, speak for themselves.

*   *   *

7: Image Setting

In January and February 1996 our team had talks about our on-field behaviour. I had learnt that some very spiteful game situations had arisen during previous seasons. I was determined that our team was not to get involved in any unsavoury acts on the field and if subjected to foul play they would move away from any incidents and perpetrations as quickly as possible. The players were not to engage in any slanging exchanges, we would endeavour to let the scoreboard results do the talking.

I am led to believe that many referees will not or do not want to get involved in women's on field distasteful acts of thuggery or verbal assaults on opposition players for fear that it may lead to a very embarrassing situation for them to be involved in a 'women's blow up' nor do they have the capacity to handle some situations. Also, an involvement of this nature could lead to a credibility factor in them losing control of the match. However, I believe that the fear that exists most is the embarrassment in being verballed by a woman or a team of women.

My players have been told, at all times they must obey and accept the referee's decision.

If any doubt of a decision existing or explanation required, it is to be exercised through the captain. Discipline in these areas must be controlled. My players have been warned if they get involved in any ugly incidents, I will remove them from the field of play. If a good sporting image is to be implemented in women's rugby it will be initiated by the Maggies.

At the completion of our first-round match against GPS the referee complemented me on the wonderful spirit in which this match was played. He added it was the best women's match he had the pleasure to referee as not one profanity was heard and the only incident, he had to reprimand any player on was an accidental high tackle on one of our players. At an after-game function I mentioned the referee's comments to the GPS coach and he replied that the referee expressed the same comments to him also. We have found a coach and team in GPS, at this point in time compatible to our way of thinking and desire to portray a good image of sportsmanship to the public, by women in rugby. We must keep on pursuing this objective.

*   *   *

Following my appointment as state coach and selector, myself and fellow selector Margariete Howard attended a game in search of potential prop forwards, our most sensitive area in the compilation of the inaugural State team. One team consisted of the competitions biggest forward pack with two potential prop forwards and their opposition had another.

Amongst the three, one prop was considered almost a certainty for a state appointment. However, in the first half, while standing on her feet, deliberately kicked an opposition player lying on the ground in the head. The referee, who was in very close proximity to the incident disbelievingly sent her off for five minutes (permissible in women's rugby). I could not believe the referees reaction to this incident. If the same offence occurred in male rugby the perpetrator would have received in instant dismissal from the field with possibly a six week plus suspension.

This incident once again supports my belief that male referees in women's rugby will not make the hard decisions, not wishing to get into any uncomfortable embarrassing situations.

I later spoke to a QRU official of the incident and the referees' reaction. The official said he would in turn speak to the appropriate people within the QRUs referees' structure.

At a later date when selecting the State squad this incident was again discussed. Were we to select a player perhaps most capable in a problem area or were we to take the hard stance on cleaning up the image of women's rugby? We took the latter option. We had to stand by our convictions ... 'deliberately kick someone in the head and get selected for Queensland?' our credibility would suffer. I spoke with the players of our decision; through this action we hoped would filter through the ranks of women's rugby.

*   *   *

8: Pre-Season Matches

In early 1996 in association with the Maggies, I was interested to know why the University of Queensland and the Barbarians were better teams and had played off in the previous grand finals. I was to learn there was little difference between the teams as most games between them were close affairs with some games resulting in nil all draws. Where Barbarians had a very large and dominating pack, which eventually wore oppositions down, in contrast University were more of the running specialists.

I also learnt, that the University president Jake Howard, a former prop for Queensland and Australia as well as an assistant coach for Australia, along with his wife Margariete had input into the University women's team and that factor alone put a gap between them and the remainder of the competition teams. Having learnt that Jake Howard had input into women's coaching and the great Bob Templeton (University, Queensland and Australian coach) often running the rule over their women's team I felt a little relieved, thinking *"That if it was good enough for Jake and Tempo ..."*

My first endeavour was to see these two teams play and observe first-hand the 'difference factor'. I saw the University team win the 'Brisbane Sevens' and the Howard input was evident with mini mauling, quick transfer of ball, continuity in play and outstanding support skills; a great advertisement for running rugby.

Our first pre-season matches were arranged against the two

teams which had dominated women's rugby in the Brisbane Barbarians and University. Barbarians had dominated other teams in Brisbane with a huge forward pack and University with a fast and expansive game. Two teams of total contrast which I felt the need to play to enable us to be adaptable and capable of playing both styles of games depending on the opposition's strengths and weaknesses. We held no fear of the Barbarians' forwards as South Maggies were producing quite a large and mobile pack themselves as will be shown in the later part of the season. However, we decided to play the running game against the Barbarians (a test of fitness and endurance progression) and a forward's game against the University team.

*   *   *

The Maggies defeated Barbarians 12-0 (two tries, one conversion) in a pretty scrappy game, which gave us much to work on prior to the University match. After observing that match, I knew the Barbarians would never be a threat to us in 1996.

Our second pre-season match against University turned into an outstanding and entertaining game. The result was beyond expectations. Here the Maggies produced a game at that stage of the season I did not believe they were capable of producing. A game consisting of one segment of five phases of play and many four phases that I believe the University team had never been subjected to; continuity and probing by an opposition. The game concluded in a 17-5 win to the Maggies (three tries, one conversion to a try against). Even though the win over University was more impressive than the one over Barbarians, I knew University was going to be our greatest challenge for the season.

* * *

A third pre-season match was arranged against Sunnybank resulting in a 22-0 victory. Three pre-season matches all on opposition grounds gave us a great deal of satisfaction. However, we realised we had deficiencies, a lot of work to do in the elimination of weaknesses while maintaining strengths.

* * *

9: A Lack of Depth

At the first club meeting I noted Souths Maggies had seventeen in attendance with three apologies, total twenty — not even enough for a team with a full complement on the bench total (total twenty-two players). Unfortunately, Souths Maggies we're not the only club short on numbers as I know other district clubs suffered also through lack of players. Souths Maggies had three shift workers, who were not always available although on most occasions they were able to adjust shifts with other work mates. At times I commenced games with fourteen players as one of our members, Sharon De Loryn a high-profile netball player having netball and rugby timings clash, would turn up for the rugby match after commencement to take her place on the wing. We have played other suburban teams fielding only fourteen players due to injured players not available. At times I have compensated by only fielding fourteen players against them.

The only team in the competition which was never affected by lack of players was University. It was explained to me by Margariete Howard that at the beginning of the season they had enough potential players turn up that they could field three teams.

I asked Margariete, *"When their playing squad was settled, why didn't the University feed the 'leftovers' out to the suburban teams lacking in numbers".*

The reply was, *"If University members could not crack their rugby team, they would seek to represent University in other sports teams"*.

The lack of playing numbers in most suburban teams was a constant concern for clubs. For Souths Maggies the lack of depth in playing numbers took a huge toll on the team in the latter part of the season.

*   *   *

10: The 'Crosby Cup'

*The 'Crosby Cup' was a pre-season
competition hosted by Brothers Rugby Club.*

All other clubs played their first round of matches on the Wednesday, Thursday and Friday nights with the exception of South Maggies and Sunnybank. Their first-round match was played at 9:00am on the Sunday morning on the day of the 'Crosby Cup' finals. Then followed by a semi-final match against Brothers at 12:35pm and in winning we went into the final of the Cup against University, the winners of the other group at 5:00pm.

The final would be University's second game for the day, Maggies third.

We started the day with twenty players, by finals time three could not take the field due to injury and another three should not have. Our three injured players were all backs and I was compelled to play a forward in the backline. Before there was the score on the board our vice-captain and lock Lisa Dwan suffered a knee injury and had to be removed from the field. Within minutes I was confronted with a more serious problem, captain Bronwyn Calvert suffered a severe hip injury and had to be carried from the field.

Another forward into the backline ... fifteen left standing.

The game was mostly controlled in the University's half. Late in the second half Bronwyn, who had been receiving treatment insisted she retake the field (permissible under 'Crosby Cup' rules). I was hesitant to support her suggestion, however following much insistence I reluctantly left the decision to her.

One injured player on, one injured player off.

A few minutes later I was confronted by Lisa Dwan with an ice pack on her knee. She said she wanted to go back on. I explained to Lisa it was impractical to send a player onto the field who could not run. Lisa immediately tore the bandage and ice pack from a knee and turning her back to me hobbled ten metres, turned and said, *"See. I can bloody well run"*. I knew she performed that stupid little demonstration under sufferance. Well, I was only replacing one injured player with another, so on went Lisa.

In the closing minutes of the game, with the score stilled locked in at nil all, Souths Maggies won a critical ruck some fifteen metres from the University's goal line and the ball was hastily passed to Pearl Palaialii, our blockbusting prop standing off the ruck, who then crashed through Uni's line of defence, passed onto supporting Bronwyn Calvert, transferred to co centre Tanya Osbourne, who scored the try being the only score of the match for the Maggies to win the 'Crosby Cup' 5-0.

Here we were elated that we had won the 'Crosby Cup', however with a string of injuries only one week out from the commencement of the 'National Mutual' competition.

It was confirmed on the 14th of April 1996 what I had suspected, in this team that the 'Southern Districts Rugby Union Football Club' did have something very special. They had by then won my total support and admiration. I felt proud to be associated with them.

'Brothers Rugby Club', the hosts for the 'Crosby Cup' presented a very small cup to the 'Maggies' for their win in the 'Trophy' final, however captain Bronwyn Calvert did not even get to touch the cup as it was explained to her that it was to remain in the Brothers Club trophy cabinet for next year's 'Crosby Cup' club presentation.

*   *   *

Souths Maggies pre-season match results:
Defeated Barbarians 12-0
Defeated University 17-5
Defeated Sunnybank 22-0
'Crosby Cup' match results:
Defeated Sunnybank 27-0
Defeated Brothers 22-0
Defeated University 5-0

*   *   *

Lisa Dwan recovered sufficiently to captain the 'Maggies' in their first competition match in lieu of Bronwyn Calvert, who along with fellow backline team mates Juliet Menzies and Marlena Phillips did not play.

A Family Affair?

Prominent rugby woman to Ailsa Woodard in April 1966:

"You know Tasi now has twenty-two daughters"

"But he's only got twenty players."

"Don't forget the manager and assistant manager."

*   *   *

11: Team Presentation

In my very early days as a young footballer (Australian Rules) our coach always insisted that our team even though may not be the best team must always present ourselves on the ground looking like a team. In those days' boots were proudly polished with nugget ending up with a nice shine then threaded with newly washed white laces. This early discipline had stuck with me through my football career and also carried into my coaching philosophy.

Personal and team presentation in any capacity became a high priority on my list.

Following the Maggies' success at the completion of the 'Crosby Cup' and enjoying our success in the beer garden, an elderly gentleman introduced himself and congratulated me on the Maggies win. He expressed his main reason was to convey that of all the women's teams (eight) at the cup, that South Maggies dress and presentation was by far the most outstanding and it was a delight to see a team run onto the pitch so well presented, an area where teams in Brisbane on all levels of club rugby were lacking.

He concluded he was pleased we won because of our presentation and we looked like a team.

I had earlier addressed this subject with the Maggies although I believe it already existed. I am sure their personal presentation was important to them for several reasons. They are women who possess a healthy vanity, but above all they possessed a pride in the club they represented and I will have no argument in the stated case they were the best presented team in all the nine grade sides that represented Southern Districts Rugby Union Football Club.

So, this was the case, when they ran onto the ground on the 21st of April 1996 for their first competition match of the season.

I can unashamedly state that I felt a touch of pride in seeing them take the field so immaculately dressed and very much looking like a professional outfit. I have no doubt, Bronwyn Calvert standing beside me felt a little of the same, however totally disappointed that it was not her leading them on.

* * *

12: Lifting the Profile

On Wednesday 24th of April I invited Souths General Manager — Anita Wilkinson, Maggies Captain — Bronwyn Calvert, Vice-Captain Lisa Dwan and also Team Manager — Gayle Hammond to my residence for dinner; a social chat and a women's rugby 'talkfest'. The appointment of Anita to General Manager of the club was one of the greatest assets to the women's cause that occurred in 1996. Over a wonderful dinner prepared by my wife Ailsa, we discussed team agenda items I had prepared. However, the main agenda item I wished to discuss was, how we could assist in raising the awareness of women's rugby, firstly within our own club, other clubs and in turn the public.

The general consensus was to initiate a more professional attitude within our own team, both in administration and on the field of play. Anita was in the position to carry out this internally through Souths Club and also into the QRU through her position in regular managerial meetings with the QRU and also with other club managers, who held meetings between themselves on a monthly basis to discuss club management problems.

* * *

It came to pass that there was a huge gap between some teams in the competition. This I believed was a lack of recognition on club level of the women's teams in not seeking or securing coaches who have a degree of competence in this field or even assisting them in obtaining qualified coaches.

I may add that we had bought this matter to notice to the QRU.

The QRU coaching personnel had assured us they had advertised to all clubs requesting for clubs to provide nominations and members to attend a 'Level One National Coaching' course with intent to coach their women's teams.

The QRU did not receive one application.

I may also add that I went to the Maggies at their request, not approached by on club level.

If it could be shown to the club's General Managers meetings that the Souths club, through Anita Wilkinson was serious in lifting the profile of women's rugby. If Souths would elevate their standard with a more professional attitude then perhaps, we would force other clubs to follow suit. This would be on two fronts, embarrassment and by being left behind in an expanding level of rugby.

By having the Maggies producing a level of rugby on a parity with the University team, one which is worthy of viewing, may cause clubs some concern of being left behind.

I may be accused of being a little hypocritical as only a few months earlier, I also like many males, felt we were losing one of our last dominions of male independence by a women's movement threatening that domain .... and here I was going in to bat for their cause.

I was starting to appreciate that they had not taken up rugby simply because it was a male's domain, but here existed many fine athletes wishing to excel in their chosen sport.

*   *   *

13: The 'National Mutual Cup'

"First Round — First Competition Match":

Here we were having played six matches prior to the season proper scoring 105 points for to 5 against but yet to have a solitary point in the 'National Mutual Cup' competition.

The competition draw saw us playing Easts in the first round.

Unfortunately for Easts, who in the first seasons had a competitive team but had been torn apart by internal problems among the players themselves, not at club level and were attempting to rebuild after a team split.

Unfortunately, they were only able to get fourteen onto the field for the Souths Maggies match and unknowingly were pitted against a team primed to explode onto the 1996 season.

The final score was disappointing and it took less than a minute for the Maggies to score the first of their eighteen tries for the match.

One had to admire the spirit of the Easts team, which although soundly thrashed battled on to the final whistle and unfortunately had one of their better players in Samantha Hughes breaking her collar bone in the last minute of the game.

Souths Maggies had won their first competition match for 1996, 114-0.

Easts women's team internal problems first came to my notice through their Vice President and after confirmed through their club General Manager, the great Grant Batty.

In speaking with Grant after the match he stated that the women's internal problems appear to have been resolved and were now on a rebuilding phase. His management committee would support and assist their women's team in development areas. Time will tell.

Our first match against Easts was ended ten minutes from full time. The referee approached me and explained they have the authority to call a game off under the clause of a 'no contest', he hoped I did not mind the game had ended short of full time.

Of course, I did not. The game was played at Easts home ground following the 'A Grade' men's match and all but family, husbands and friends had left the venue.

At the following training session several Souths' supporters approached me asking the women's game results. When told the Maggies had won 114-0 in a shortened match their disbelief was evident, with the most common reaction, *"Women cannot score 100 points in a game!"*

My reply was, *"Why don't you come and see them play?"*

                           *   *   *

"First Round — Second Competition Match":

In the Maggies first home game for the season against GPS we experienced an introduction to playing in the wet, muddy and cold conditions. This experience gave us an opportunity to enter into a new dimension ... wet weather rugby.

Perhaps the most comforting issue was that now quite a large crowd had elected to stay and watch a game played in drizzling rain and muddy conditions, perhaps out of curiosity more than for the spectacle. This inquisitiveness at the time, no doubt emanating by word of mouth that the Souths club did possess a women's team that was capable of playing a running, expansive game worthy of spectacle. It is noteworthy that the women's games are played following the 'A Grade' men's game whereby most spectators retired to the clubhouse or go home. It was a revelation to see a reasonable spectator crowd remain for the women's match. Perhaps our approach was starting to get through to the rugby public ... women can play rugby.

Left: Wendy Packer from 'GPS Rugby' is a very impressive No8/Lock and in retrospect should have been selected in the inaugural Queensland women's team in 1996.

Even under the conditions the spectators were subjected to, the Maggies left no doubt that they were a very good running and defensive unit. By half time they had scored five tries to lead 31-0. They scored another three tries in the second half to win their second competition match 50-0.

For the first time in 1996 the Maggies had a reserve back for the game with the return from injury of captain Bronwyn Calvert. The centre pairing of Bronwyn and Tanya Osbourne is equalled only by

University pair in Bronwyn Laidlaw and Cathy Boulton. Between them they scored six tries, three each. GPS has the basis of a good team and possess an outstanding and imposing player in their No8 Wendy Packer. Wendy was an impressive athlete and certainly was instrumental in relieving the Maggies of a great deal of ruck/maul possession. It was not as if the Maggies have not been subjected to the importance of ball security and retention, it was indicative of this fine rugby player's ability in the art of tight play. Wendy was among the best players on the field. That observation was supported in an after games function, where she was announced as player of the match, by Souths. In making that announcement it was commented by long time Souths male supporter, *"It is good to see the women's team bringing some good old-time values back into the club."*

*   *   *

"First Round — Third Competition Match" — The Taste of Defeat :

Onto the premiers of the first seasons of women's rugby in Brisbane. As mentioned previously, the Queensland University team field one very efficient, athletic team and carry very huge numbers in depth and can only admire their philosophy towards 'the running game'. University were capable of playing the expansive game and I in turn was determined by the end of the season to close that gap.

Souths Maggies as with most other Brisbane teams carry a small squad. In our case we had twenty players however, fortunately our spare five were very good players so to a degree we did carry strength in depth, necessitating rotation of players.

With a 5-5 score line at half time and with the resumption of play for the first eight to ten minutes we pressured the University line and I believed we would finally overwhelm them. However, with grit and determination they held out the Maggies then through a series of ball retention moves and support play eventually moved play to the Maggies' twenty-five where they kicked a penalty goal to break the deadlock. University finished the game with a fine team try to run out eventual winners 13-5 thus inflicting the first defeat on the Maggies for 1996. This game reinforced my earlier belief that University was the team we had to defeat to win a premiership.

*   *   *

Following games against Brothers 37-0, Sunnybank 13-0 and Wests 45-5 followed with the disappointment in having Wests score against us ... the second team to do so in 1996.

The final of the first round loomed as the battle of the heavyweights, Barbarians, the grand finalist of the first seasons of women's rugby and the Maggies no doubt the next largest pack in the competition. It was a game to be hosted by the Maggies who were looking forward to the confrontation, as by now Maggies had themselves created quite a formidable pack both in size and forward structures applicable to 'Unit 1 and 2' capabilities. In an amazing clash of the two biggest packs in Brisbane women's rugby was something to behold as it was beyond my comprehension that two women's teams could produce such a forwards' clash without inflicting a huge injury toll on each other.

The Maggies backline was overall superior scoring tries in

both halves, the first in a 60-metre break by Bronwyn Calvert and the second by the backline completing a move from forward phase play and outflanking a depleted opposition for winger Charlie Beitzel to casually score following a great to build up. Tanya Osbourne converted following a first half penalty goal to give the Maggies a 15-0 win to complete the competition's first round of matches.

This game left no doubt that the Maggies now had the dominant pack of forwards within the competition.

Note: This pack consisting of:

Front Row: Moana O'Rourke, Bronwyn Hart and Pearl Palaialii became a Queensland front row with Pearl Palaialii and Bronwyn Hart both representing Australia.

Second Row: Lisa Dwan and Anna Maccheroni with Lisa Dwan representing both Queensland and Australia. Anna Maccheroni would not have looked out of place in a Queensland pack.

Back Row ('Unit 2' forwards): Consisting of Selena Worsley, Shirley Russell both representing Queensland and Australia, Kelly Edmunds, Shelley Hancock with Amanda Dinsdale lock or backrow. Amanda was more often than not used in the backline such was her versatility and a lack of backline numbers. Amanda represented Queensland in 1997 such was her ability.

*   *   *

Following the first round of matches the Maggies were second on the competition ladder after University's undefeated round.

The Maggies' statistics after round one:
Versus Easts Won 114-0

Versus GPS Won 50-0

Versus University Lost 5-13

Versus Brothers Won 37-0

Versus Sunnybank Won 15-0

Versus Wests Won 45-5

Versus Barbarians Won 15-0

Points for: 281 Points against: 18

Tries for: 42 Tries against: 3

*   *   *

14: Game Analysis

Following every match, trial or competition we had a game analysis at our next training session. I speak on our positives and negatives and areas where we must concentrate on individually, unit or team. I then request the captain, vice-captain then players to have input into the analysis.

Rugby is a team game therefore it should be a team analysis.

I believe the players appreciate the opportunity to air their opinions in constructive debate. So, following constructive analysis we then train on the areas of concern.

Having told the players from day one I am approachable and any problem areas that exist they are requested to bring them to me. Almost all the team and I have had over time individual discussions mainly pertaining to their game in general or areas of other concern.

In all areas I have been honest to their concerns and even if a little hurt is created, I believe they appreciate the honesty. However, I learnt years ago you never lie to women.

* * *

15: Second Round of Matches

In hosting Easts in the second round of the competition, unfortunately Easts forfeited the game. This was very disappointing as it is now meant that players would be two weeks without a game and some three. The Maggies received four points for the forfeiture plus the best margin of points 'for & against' of the other matches played that weekend. In an amazing round the Barbarians and University drew 0-0, Wests and GPS drew 5-5 and Brothers and Sunnybank drew 10-10.

*　　*　　*

Our second-round match against GPS had to be deferred as eight of the Maggies (six forwards and two backs) were in the Queensland team and were not permitted to play that weekend due to the provincial match against Alberta (Canada) the following Tuesday at Ballymore.

Deferment of these matches is permissible if through representative selection, your team is depleted. With team members now only nineteen in total we had eleven players only available. This was a poor build up following the Easts forfeiture for the second-round clash against premiers University only two weeks away. Our game against Sunnybank resulted in a 35-0 win.

*　　*　　*

A large crowd witnessed the Maggies University clash and the game lived up to expectations. The Maggies were the first to score with outstanding backline ball skills and with fullback Karen Turner's insertion into the backline, showing a clean pair of heels scored with Tanya Osbourne converting. Early in the second half young 19-year-old prop Margie Cummins scored an unconverted try from a set move giving the Maggies are very comfortable 12-0 lead. In the closing stages of the game University with a continuous supply of ball from outstanding phase play eventually found the gap that enabled them to score next to the uprights and convert to bring the full-time score of a Maggies 12-7 victory.

I was informed it was the first time in the 'National Mutual Cup' competition that the Maggies had defeated Queensland University since the initiation of women's rugby in Brisbane.

This win placed the Maggies on top of the ladder due to University's draw with the Barbarians some three weeks earlier.

We had a break in this competition due to the 'Queensland Club' competition.

*   *   *

Following deferment of club games due to the Queensland State side attending the first Interstate Cup Championship held in Sydney and on returning from Sydney on Sunday morning the 21st July, our State players once off the aircraft went to the Souths Club and filled in the holes to get fifteen on the ground.

During the absence of eight players and myself the remainder of the team was left in the capable hands of veteran player Charlie Beitzel to coach in our absence and was responsible for team selection on our return. She designated the holes to fill by State players on arrival at Souths venue.

Five State players were used in the game against Wests; however, the game was comfortably won 38-7. Five State players had just completed five games in a week . Our next game was against the Barbarians ending in a nil all draw. To complete our second-round matches against Brothers and GPS winning then 12-0 and 65-0 respectively

*　　*　　*

We had an undefeated second round — at the completion of this round of matches:
Versus Easts who Forfeited
Versus Sunnybank Won 35-0
Versus University Won 12-7
Versus Wests Won 38-7
Versus Barbarians Draw 0-0
Versus Brothers Won 12-0
Versus GPS Won 65- 0

Points for: 162 Points against: 14
Tries for: 29 Tries against: 2

*　　*　　*

Souths Maggies after two rounds now possessed an outstanding record of:
Points for: 443 Points against: 32
Tries for: 71 Tries against: 5

16: Queensland Club Competition

The 'Queensland Club Championship' was played by teams from North Queensland, Central Queensland and the eight Brisbane clubs. In pool matches the Maggies defeated GPS 72-0 and Barbarians 15-3 and was to meet University in the championship final. In a hard-fought game with intensity by both teams the game moved from one goal line to the other. Finally, the Maggies received and kicked a penalty goal to win the final 3-0. Typical of all contests between these two teams no quarter was given nor asked with nothing separating the quality of both teams.

"These two teams play at a level of intensity that no other club sides in Australia are capable of." This was passed on to me at the conclusion of the State Club Championship on the 10th of June 1996 by a visiting dignitary from the Australian Institute of Sports (A.I.S.) Canberra.

The final caused injuries to four State players, two from each team which was a worry, however none proved to be long term thankfully as the Queensland team was departing for Sydney the following weekend for the first Interstate Championship.

Due to these Championships our next game versus Brothers had to be deferred.

*　　*　　*

17: Third Round of Matches

Round 3 was disappointing. Of our seven scheduled games, three games were forfeited with some district teams, through injuries and not able to put full strength teams on the field.

However, once again the third-round match against University building up to the finals was looked forward to with great anticipation.

University edged the Maggies 10-5 to give them wins in Rounds 1 and 3 with the Maggies winning in Round 2.

The Maggies ended Round 3 amassing '51 points for to 10 points against' in their four games. With the Maggies losing to University in Round 3, University completed the competition rounds as Minor Premiers.

Souths Maggies progressive total for 1996:

Points for: 493 Points against: 42
Tries for: 78 Tries against: 7

*   *   *

Chapter 18: The Finals
– The 'National Mutual Cup'

The four teams as predicted to make up the 1996 finals were:

1: University of Queensland
2: Souths Maggies
3: Norths Barbarians
4: Brothers

Sunnybank pressed Brothers for fourth position, however a huge gap stood between the top three and the remaining five teams. In the minor semi-final Barbarians easily accounted for Brothers 31-0.

With the Maggies playing ranks now standing at eighteen we were not in the position of having depth in our reserves but still the belief existed in those remaining.

In our last training session prior to playing University in the major semi-final, with the winner automatically going into the grand final, I talked in depth to the advantages of going directly into the grand final and also disadvantages of not playing a game for a fortnight prior to a grand final. This subject I'm sure has been debated over for generations.

My main concern, however with our playing ranks now down to eighteen, going straight into the grand final would certainly delete an extra game in losing and then having to play in the preliminary final against the Barbarians.

University of Queensland defeated Souths Maggies 8-0 in the major semi-final to go directly into the grand final.

My real concern for the loss was the huge penalty count incurred by the Maggies, an area we as a team had to address at our next training session.

Preliminary Final:

Reviewing our loss to University we decided to bring veteran player Charly Bietzel from the wing into the five-eighth position. Charly had represented Australia in a 1995 test against New Zealand, was perhaps our fittest player, better defensive and gave our inside backs a slicker service. She would be playing inside two Queensland (soon to be Australian) centres in Bronwyn Calvert and Tanya Osbourne. This positional change was suggested by the senior players within the team; however, it was up to me to make the announcement. I took the incumbent five-eighth aside and tried to explain this decision was for the benefit of the team. She broke up, however no tears, shouting or putting on a huge tantrum would change my mind. She quit the Maggies vowing to no longer train or play with them. Our numbers were now down to seventeen.

* * *

As with previous games against the Barbarians there was no huge difference in the score as was the case in matches previously played in 1996. These games were always absorbing as the two teams possess the biggest and strongest forwards in perhaps Australian women's club rugby. The forwards would generally negate each other; however, the backline skills, pace and defence of the Maggies backs was decidedly the difference. Two tries scored by the backs, the first following a breach of the opposition's backline sending captain Bronwyn Calvert on a sixty-metre run to the try line and the second by co centre Tanya Osbourne. Both tries unconverted with the Maggies winning a rugged game 10-0.

My last team talk before game commencement was simply, *"You win this game today and I will show you how to win a grand final, that I promise."*

* * *

Right: Stand in coach, veteran Charly Bietzel played a prominent role in the 'Maggies' Preliminary and Grand Final wins.

The negative aspects of playing in a preliminary final came to the fore as early in the game as one of our versatile and outstanding backs, Sharon De Loryn suffered a head injury, a bad eye socket bone fracture.

Sharon as with her attitude refused to come off the field,

however it was to deny her a grand final appearance, her season ended one game short. More bad news following a badly broken nose to our young Queensland prop Moana O'Rourke, nineteen years of age was not allowed to play in the grand final by her mother. The Maggies' ranks had now shrunk to fifteen players.

*   *   *

Coming from the field following the Barbarians match one Maggies player exclaimed as realisation set in, *"Shit! We are in a grand final"* ... their first.

*   *   *

19: Grand Final
'The National Mutual Cup' 1996

'Lead up':

University were playing for consecutive crowns and deserved favourites to retain their crown following consecutive defeats of Souths Maggies in their last two clashes, 10-5 and 8-0.

We trained the usual Tuesday and Thursday evenings; however, I included a session for the Saturday afternoon on the Eve of the grand final.

Our squad consisted of nine forwards and six backs.

Left: Amanda Dinsdale (left) and Debbie Grylls.
Amanda was a Backrow Forward/Lock for Souths and was forced onto the wing for the Grand Final scoring the first try of that match. She represented Queensland in 1997.

Debbie was 'Maggies' Halfback and selected in the Queensland 1997 squad. From there she represented Australia in the same year.

*   *   *

We had Amanda Dinsdale a fit athletic backrow amongst our forwards. Amanda possessed a turn of speed with good ball skills so Amanda was moved to the wing to operate outside two Queensland centres (soon to be Australian centres) in captain Bronwyn Calvert and Tanya Osbourne. With Debbie Grylls (chosen in the Queensland 1997 squad, that promotion eventually led to her Australian elevation also in 1997) at halfback and

with Charly Beitzel at five-eighth amounted to a strong backline, which was supported by a very speedy fullback in Karen Turner and the ever-reliable Julie Menzies on the other wing.

We had to be strong in this area as University's strength lay in their backs with six representing Queensland and four of them to be Australian representatives. University's forwards also could not be ignored with four of them representing Queensland and two of them in Deena Aitken and Mieke Gladwin, being Australian representatives.

Saturday afternoon's

Right: Locks Anna Maccheroni (left) and Lisa Dwan (V/Captain) gave the 'Maggies' size and power. Lisa was a Queensland and Australian Lock while Anna would not be out of place in a Queensland pack.

session was a full team run consisting of our reshuffled team. In the forwards after losing young Queensland prop Moana O'Rourke (badly broken nose) our pack had to be readjusted. Having two-thirds of a Queensland and Australian front row in Pearl Palaialii prop and hooker Bronwyn Hart in our ranks I moved Bronwyn (her suggestion) to the loose head front row and replaced the hooking position with Shelley Handcock, a tenacious and hard-working breakaway.

Our locks in Lisa Dwan (Queensland and Australian forward) with Anna Maccheroni remained and our backrow of two breakaways in Selena Worsley and Shirley Russell (both Queensland and Australian reps) were supported by No8 Kellie Edmunds.

Above: 'Maggies' Props and Hookers (L-R): Bronwyn Hart (Hooker), Moana O'Rourke (Prop), Margie Cummins (Prop), Kirsty Taylor (Hooker), Pearl Palaialii (Prop).

Unfortunately, only two made it to the Grand Final though both being Queensland and Australian representatives, Bronwyn Hart and Pearl Palaialii. Moana O'Rourke, a nineteen-year-old

Queensland Prop had to withdraw from the Grand Final with a badly broken nose suffered during the Preliminary Final.

Above: 'Maggies' four Backrow Forwards (L-R): Selena Worsley, Amanda Dinsdale, Shelley Handcock and Shirley Russell.

Amanda was moved to the wing for the Grand Final and Shelley for her first game as a Hooker. Selena Worsley (Australia's best defensive Breakaway) and fellow Breakaway Shirley Russell are both Queensland and Australian representatives.

We retained a big mobile pack which I believed, providing we had no injuries would eventually get on top of the University pack.

* * *

It was from this Saturday session that I sensed an 'air' of confidence, without being arrogant in their attitude. I went away from that final session comfortable in my assessment that Souths Maggies were going to win their first grand final. This team confidence I first detected prior to winning the 'Crosby Cup' and also the 'Queensland Women's Club Championship', both against University earlier in the season.

I felt secure in the knowledge that the current premiers would have to produce their finest to continue their undefeated grand final wins.

*   *   *

Our grand final team submitted to the QRU for publication was:

1: Bronwyn Hart	9: Debbie Grylls
2: Shelley Handcock	10: Charlie Bietzel
3: Pearl Palaialii	11: Julie Menzies
4: Lisa Dwan (Vice-Captain)	12: Bronwyn Calvert (Captain)
5: Anna Maccheroni	13: Tanya Osbourne
6: Shirley Russell	14: Amanda Dinsdale
7: Selena Worsley	15: Karen Turner
8: Kellie Edmunds	Tasi Woodard (Coach)

*   *   *

'Grand Final':

> *"If you break an arm you cannot come off; if you break a leg I will come on and carry you off"* ... my last words to South Maggies before they ran onto the field.

With envy I looked at the University's reserved bench where there were seven to eight of them. I looked at South's bench opposite, we had none.

I sat in the grandstand with my wife Ailsa. Margariete Howard with Bob Templeton accompanying her came and sat two seats in front of us. I knew Margariete Howard was going to speak to me again if University won the grand final.

I wondered if she thought, *"Why isn't Woodard, being the Maggies coach not down with his reserves?"*

We had none.

I wondered, *"Would we be the only rugby union team in the world to play in a grand final without a reserve player?"*

* * *

Following is a roundup of the Brisbane Women's Rugby grand final 1996 by an independent correspondent:

'Maggies Magic'

"Souths Maggies won their first grand final; University of Queensland lost their first grand final."

"Souths Maggies defeated premiers University 15 points to 8 in an excellent match, which saw Maggies more committed pack eventually wear down their opposition forwards in a tough encounter and eventually their backs putting the 'icing on the cake' in polishing off University with two outstanding tries.

The backs were also totally committed in defence shutting down many University backline sorties before gaining momentum.

The Maggies drew first blood with a great long-range penalty by centre Osbourne. University replied with a penalty goal, which saw the game locked up at 3-3 by half time.

Ten minutes into the second half saw the fierce defensive game start to take toll on the University forwards and an ascendancy was becoming evident. From sideline phase play the Maggies backs attacked and winger Amanda Dinsdale was prominent in scoring the first try of the match, which was converted by Osbourne given the Maggies a 10-3 lead. Again, Maggies worked their way into the University twenty-five from the kick off. They put the game to rest with a wonderful back line passage of play enabling fullback Karen Turner to seal the grand final with an unconverted try and a lead of 15-3.

University through their backline probed relentlessly, however due to the defence of Australia's most dynamic defensive breakaway Selena Worsley, they were cut down in a display one would not have thought possible by a woman.

Eventually University scored a try in the final thirty seconds of play for a full-time score of 15-8."

*　　*　　*

Was history made? Were Souths Maggies the first rugby team in history to participate in and win a grand final without a reserve player?

Margariete Howard with Bob Templeton left the grandstand. Passing me Margariete kept her word ... she never spoke to me again.

At the conclusion of the game in me thanking the University coach he asked, *"How did you do that?"*

"We played through your weaknesses," I replied.

He looked at me and said, *"Didn't know we had any."*

The grand final presentation took place on the Ballymore pitch with captain Bronwyn Calvert accepting the 'National Mutual Cup' from the QRU official then making her speech.

I noticed the University team seated on the turf near the pitch exit and noted some sobbing while team mates attempted to console them. I admired the University team and could sympathise with them having at last losing supremacy in that they were regarded as the best club side in Australia.

Following the presentation, I went under the grandstand to join the Maggies in celebration in their change room. Firstly, I had to pass the University change room and I was going to enter and thank them for the game as many of their players were dear to me, ten in fact with whom I coached in the inaugural Queensland team. However, as I neared their change room I halted as they were receiving a very loud, and I presume tongue lashing by Margariete Howard for their loss. Hearing this tirade saddened me as once again I state they are a marvellous team and if in fact it was, did not deserve a verbal assault.

Above: 'Maggies' Captain Bronwyn Calvert accepting the 'National Mutual Trophy' from a QRU official and then making a winning speech.

I went onto the Maggies dressing room where the atmosphere was one, I can assure you, more pleasant. Not one club official from Souths bothered to visit their club's grand final winning team.

*   *   *

At the conclusion of the 1996 season 'Souths Maggies' had won the trifecta:

1: Trophy Holders – 'Crosby Cup'

2: Title Winners – 'Queensland Women's Club Championship'

3: Premiers – 'The National Mutual Cup'

*   *   *

'The National Mutual Cup'

Played 18: Won 14   Lost 3   Drawn 1

Points for: 519   Points against: 58

Tries for: 81   Tries against: 9

*   *   *

'All Other Matches'

Played 9: Won 9

Points for: 195   Points against: 8

*   *   *

1996 — Total points for: 714 Points against: 66

'SOUTHS MAGGIES' 1996

*Back Row (L-R): Megan Walton, Lee Ann O'Brien,
Charly Bietzel, Shelley Handcock*

*Centre Row (L-R): Sharyn De Loryn, Julie Menzies, Kellie Edmunds,
Anna Maccheroni, Amanda Dinsdale, Moana O'Rourke*

*Front Row (L-R): Shirley Russell, Karen Turner, Debbie Grylls,
Tasi Woodard (Coach), Bronwyn Calvert (Captain), Tanya Osbourne,
Selena Worsley*

Absent: Lisa Dwan (Vice-Captain), Bronwyn Hart, Pearl Palaialii.

*   *   *

20: A Sad Chapter for 1996/1997

Souths 'A Grade' men's team, one of the strongest club teams in the world, possessing seven current Wallabies and eleven Queensland representatives were odds on to win their sixth consecutive grand final, surpassing the five 'won on the trot' by the great Brothers teams of the late 70s and early 80s.

The 'Maggies' (the Souths 'A Grade' women's team) were the first senior side to win South's a grand final in 1996, followed by Souths 'Colts'. In perhaps the upset of the decade GPS defeated Souths 'A Grade' men's in the grand final.

On Souths' trophy and presentation night 'Souths Maggies' were represented by twelve players and myself, however the night was poorly attended with only two 'A Grade' men's players present. It was the smallest trophy night attendance that old time supporters could remember and certainly one of low key.

In the President's speech he remarked of the great disappointment in the 'A Grade' men's not securing their sixth premiership. However, he went onto acknowledge that their 'Colts' team had won an outstanding grand final. The President on finalising his speech to wrap up the season resumed his seat.

Several committee members went over and spoke in his ear at a probable oversight. He moved again to the rostrum and added, "Oh ... and congratulations to the women in winning their grand final," and again resumed his seat.

Here was a team that won the club's first grand final for 1996, produced eight State representatives for their club and seven of those Australian representatives, not one mention of these achievements. I knew the women felt absolutely neglected which had been apparent in the relationship over the season.

I also felt let down by Souths in general … they failed to recognise the women's outstanding season.

Bronwyn Calvert had told me previously they had almost walked out on the club due to a very embarrassing and indecent incident perpetrated on them at the end of the '95 season, mentioned previously in this book.

At the conclusion of the '96 season I told the team I would not be coaching them in 1997 although through the club, ensure they would get at least a 'Level One' coach for them. I would continue coaching them in the pre-season period until a satisfactory coach was procured.

Before and during the '97 pre-season period, Bronwyn told me several of the players were going to either retire or move onto another club due to the lack of support by Souths to their women's team. At the end of January '97 there was much unrest within the team so I had a team meeting in the major change room and requested them to:

Not to disintegrate or if some team members felt that they had to leave, all go together to keep the team intact.

I reminded them that they now possessed currently eight State players and seven Internationals due to being in such a successful team.

Further to this, that I also would support them if they as a team decided to relocate to another club. With that I left the meeting.

On leaving the meeting I was confronted by a very senior club official wanting to speak to me, *"Tasi, I hear a rumour that the women are contemplating on leaving the club. Can you stop them as without them we cannot win a Club Championship?"*

I thought, suddenly the 'Southern Districts Rugby Union' Club through their women's team have just realised they have an asset.

I replied, *"The situation is out of my hands. It is their decision on their future."*

Within the Brisbane competition Kenmore, a very strong previous second division club were promoted to the Brisbane reserve grade competition in 1996 and in winning that premiership was promoted to the 'National Mutual Cup' competition along with the Gold Coast in expanding the Brisbane competition in 1997.

If the Maggies were to relocate to another club this was the opportunity as it meant going to a new club without a women's team and in turn, they would not be displacing current players within existing women's team.

If the team was to move, I would support their intent and also continue their pre-season coaching until Kenmore can produce an acceptable coach. When Souths heard of the persistent rumours of them losing their women's team it did cause some concern.

A delegation of women had approached the Kenmore Club of the possible relocation of their team and Kenmore were overwhelmed that they may inherit a premier women's team. Negotiations were still underway of the probable but still undecided move when the University club sponsored a 'Down Under Tens' competition in February with only four women's teams to be included, University, Souths, a combined Brisbane team and a Gold Coast team. Souths Maggies accepted the invitation, however the Souths Club management insisted that no player within the club could represent Souths in 1997 before becoming a fully paid financial member. Individual club player's fees were to be a huge $200 (up from $150 in 1996).

That demand put the final nail in the coffin. 'South Maggies' had played their last game. Kenmore inherited a premier team. My support went with the women.

Kenmore had several coaches within their club willing to take the women on a full-time basis.

Kenmore fielded a women's team in the 'Down Under Tens' which they eventually won defeating hosts University.

Sadly, from 'Souths Maggies' Premiership team fullback Karen Turner who was pencilled in to join the Queensland 1997 team left rugby and went to soccer … a loss for the women's rugby movement.

*   *   *

Jungle Green and Rugby

*J*ungle Green and Rugby is the second book currently being written by author CW (Tasi) Woodard, which will be available later this year.

The book unfolds his life story, being born on a remote Bass Strait island at the end of the great depression and prior to the initiation of World War Two. Virtually living off the land becomes his existence for the first ten years of life; hunting for food, living on rainwater, no electricity or riding in a car. With little schooling, education came from the land, the elements, hard work and the family.

Tasi's family heritage on both sides is traced back to convict stock.

His families' military history discloses detail of the ten members, which involved service in World War One and World War Two. Knowing he was always going to be a soldier, the book delves into Tasi's own military service of twenty-six years during  both peace time and warfare, with six years' service in southeast Asia, Malaysia and Vietnam.

Such was army life, the author's post military service attendance included involvement in the 100th anniversary (2018) of the battles on the Western Front with a presentation to the Mayor of Montbrehain, France (the village reclaimed in General Monash's last conflict of World War One utilising the Australian Imperial Forces), dawn services at both Gallipoli and Villers Bretonneux, which included a wreath laying ceremony at Menin Gate Ypres Belgium, upon invitation on behalf of Australia.

Interlaced with this is a rugby career that extended over forty years, both in a service and civilian capacity, which was unintentionally initiated in the Army in 1957 and concluded in the end chapter of this book that you are holding in your hands.

The book details the many stories of Tasi's involvement as a player, player/coach, coach and manager of local and representative military rugby in both the northern and southern hemispheres. This then transpired into civilian rugby which included a tenure as Director of Coaching for a successful local rugby club. Insightfully at another layer, Tasi shares the creation and his Australian involvement with the development and subsequent proliferation of the Veterans and Golden Oldies Rugby movement.

The traveling experience of the author covers six continents with much of it being rugby related, however does cover numerous other sporting experiences. It involves some of the world's great and renowned sporting identities with Tasi being entertained by some.

Be ready for a photographic and emotive journey such is the diversity and detail of this read. Factual, historical, political, sporting, humorous and sad, which reaches out to an age group from the 1930s to the twenty first century.

Lightning Source UK Ltd.
Milton Keynes UK
UKHW020858070821
388412UK00007B/234